Contents

Introduction

The background to the book

Heads of year or house must often feel that they are characters in search of a role. Worse, some will feel that the expectations of colleagues, pupils and parents trap them in a role they find dissatisfying. The writer of this simple-minded book is neither so arrogant, nor detached from complex realities, as to claim it provides them with a role, but hopes that it will give readers the confidence to begin to clarify, and then negotiate, a meaningful role. The approach used in Chapter 1 shows how deeply the actions of heads of year and house are influenced by the conflicting expectations and perceptions of senior management and class teachers. Their relationships with academic heads are ambivalent and ambiguous in many schools, creating further complications. As a first step they will, *as a team*, have to invest considerable preparatory work into finding out how they, in the context of their own school, can engage in a dynamic and co-operative process of constructive role-making and role-taking. It is almost paradoxical that they must be a team with boundaries before they can co-operate meaningfully with other groups.

They could well begin by asking if *they* are a team. It will be easy for them to delude themselves. If they feel they are, the question posed by Adair (1986), 'Why does the team exist?', has to be tackled. If the answer is negative, then the exploration of both the explicit and less obvious causes of this is imperative. They may end by feeling that the potential benefits are outweighed by the costs of shaping themselves into a middle-management team. But at least they should be able to justify the decision: perhaps appreciating that they could steadily become an irrelevance in modern secondary education. If they decide they are, or should become, a team, then they should set out vigorously to investigate how in collaboration with other groups, especially heads of academic departments, they can help the school achieve its educational objectives.

Deputy heads should provide leadership and orientation during this initial exploration and analytic phase. The pastoral heads are not relegated to passivity; the deputies set out to encourage initiative and encourage the development of expertise. Their aim should be the facilitation of division of labour in the team with consequent inter-dependence as a prelude to effective team development. A simple principle is at work: before pastoral heads can lead and 'manage' others, they must learn the art of self-management in a team context.

Each school is a unique social system with its own constellation of strengths and problems, producing a characteristic culture and set of beliefs which deeply influence the perceptions and behaviours of those working within it. Insiders blindly adapt, taking for granted what outsiders see as problematical. This was very clear when I sent experienced teachers on attachment to schools during full-time training courses. Some returned shaking, saying with insufferable virtue, 'Do you know what goes on in that school? It is incredibly stupid!'. Gazing at them benevolently, I would get them to look at the possibility that equally inane practices might be occurring in their own schools, but as insiders caught up in the rush of school life they were blind to them. Application of the basic counselling principle that problems can only be comprehended accurately, and coped with successfully, when treated with due reference to their context is therefore essential. As usual, the poets get there first, and express it more strikingly. Eliot (1949) in *The Cocktail Party* writes:

> But before I treat a patient like yourself
> I need to know a great deal more about him,
> Than the patient himself can always tell me.
> Indeed, it is often the case that my patients
> Are only pieces of a total situation
> Which I have to explore. The single patient
> Who is ill by himself, is rather the exception.

As it is for the patient, so it is for the pastoral heads. Any attempt to provide recipes or global prescriptions is foredoomed to impotence.

A state of drift is not being advocated. The facts of adolescent development as currently interpreted, the growing awareness of creative, liberating approaches to management and organisational development are only two of the major elements contributing to the framework within which pastoral heads negotiate their role amongst

Preface

This preface is a valediction: it may even appear to be a benediction, but that would be intolerable piety. May I offer my good wishes to all those who will continue to labour to make pastoral care a meaningful reality in British schools. It is heartening that there are so many better equipped than I who will continue to work in the field. My admiration for the work done by the National Association for Pastoral Care in Education is profound. I say this as one who stood apart from it in order to maintain an independent, critical stance. Every teacher who values pastoral activity should take up active membership. If pastoral care is to meet the challenge of accelerating change in education positively, then the support and initiatives offered by NAPCE are crucial.

Special thanks to Basil Blackwell, whose qualities of gentlemanliness have survived alongside their efficiency in a thrusting, restless age. This is not sexist, for I see the quality as belonging to both sexes. Special thanks to Rodney Pollock who has done so much to support conferences and lecture courses in pastoral care: it was appreciated, Rodney.

My work has been greatly eased by the efficiency and help of Miss Frances Wood and her fellow librarians at the Education Library at Hendrefoilan. They responded to my inadequacies with competence, taking considerable trouble to obtain materials. Closely rivalling them are Miss Marjorie Bocking and her colleagues at the Cambridge Institute of Education Library. My thanks to you all. One source of support over the years has been the secretaries and porters at Hendrefoilan. Their concern, interest and friendliness have lightened the burden: it has always been good to see them as I tottered into the Department.

Mrs Letty Johns has typed the manuscript with zeal and accuracy. She dealt with my quibbles cheerfully and helpfully. My thanks are sincere, Letty.

Finally, I can only accept my limitations. The old schoolmaster's verdict, 'Trying, but could do better', may be all too accurate. Certainly, the faults and weaknesses of the book are mine alone.

Swansea,
February, 1989

themselves and – equally important – with other groups. Unfortunately, knowledge of both areas is depressingly limited in some schools. Schools where the head adopts the monarchic role – as described by Jones (1987) – or deludes himself or herself that he or she is Zeus may well be marked by such paucity of knowledge. In the latter role any Zeuses should remind themselves that the subordinate gods conspire against them: a fact that will hamper attempts at development of pastoral care.

A prominent theme in the book is therefore the need to understand, and cope with, the distorted and conflicting perceptions held by groups of the motives and standpoints of other groups within the institution. Pastoral heads must not delude themselves that they are exempt from this tendency. Eliot (1957) records his gratitude for being forced to look analytically at what he had ignored, or not recognised. He admitted he examined certain issues with 'eyes clouded with prejudice'. Adair (1986) mentions the mistrust that exists between groups, asking one to ponder on the possibility that, 'Groups on the same side are often like islands addressing each other across a sea of misunderstanding.' Some may be tempted to deny the conflicts of perception and the attribution of adverse or unprofessional intent that underlies everyday interaction in their school. Yet in the last five years, students undertaking staff development work with my guidance have repeatedly reported their existence and impact on their work. An essential step for a pastoral team contemplating development is to comprehend the intensity of these misconceptions, and assess the vested interests which make for reluctance to change them.

Another perspective taken in the discussion and exercises in this book is that it is both naïve and destructive to label colleagues as unco-operative and resistant to change. Pastoral heads may be creating resistance unintentionally by not recognising that their actions diminish the tutor's role or threaten the already insecure individual. To condemn people or groups in this crude way merely polarises positions. Developers have to take the standpoints of the alleged 'resisters', and appreciate what lies behind their attitudes and behaviour. (This does not deny the existence of the rare lazy individual who has to be 'carried' by others or that there are teachers who are inadequate or possess personality difficulties. They have to be dealt with as a professional problem by senior management.) Premature labelling of colleagues as unco-operative, or failure to appreciate that resistance could stem from inadequate explanation of change, a proper anxiety about the danger of erosion of standards, or lack of credibility by those urging the changes, is inept, even provocative. Developers are blinded by their insecurity, tendency to early closure on problems, and the refusal to admit conflicting evidence, as surely as are those about whom they complain.

Cultism is an ever-present danger in pastoral activity. Blind endorsement of active learning, over-zealous advocation of particular methods such as role-play or of a particular scheme of work for the pastoral programme, ignore the fact that there is no right way. The poor training and insecurity of pastoral heads makes them prey to fashion and persuasive influences. They search avidly for *the right way*. A blanket solution to complex problems is a delightful thought but it is still an illusion. This book stresses not so much *what* is done, but *how* it is done, and the *meaning* of that action in a context of conflicting forces. We all know there are appropriate or inappropriate behaviours in different contexts; the same behaviour has different meaning and impact in different contexts. Heads of year or house are not only searching for an appropriate role in a particular setting; but for the meaning of pastoral activity. Pastoral heads, however, give meaning to pastoral work as surely as teachers allocate significance to pupils' classroom behaviours, or the reactions of society to minorities' behaviours create deviant identities. This is compounded by their failure to see the contradictions between what they claim pastoral care is about, and the reality of day-to-day trivialities they actually emphasise in tutor work. Small wonder that many creative teachers see it as fatuous.

This emphasis on meaning and the dynamics of pastoral development is a concomitant of the fact that there is no ultimate form of pastoral care towards which we should be moving. Its forms and purposes will change as the school system changes. The social context of the school gives actions their meanings and determines their effects. Recipes are inadequate: there is no right blend of task orientation and relationship orientation or a particular management/ leadership style that can be used as a tool to cover every situation. There are ones which are appropriate with particular individuals or groups at a specific time in a situation occurring within the value climate of a unique school.

The abiding elements are the ethical principles of respectful caring for individuals, the preservation of proper confidentiality, and the duty critically and constantly to scrutinise our motives and purposes. This is all the more compelling because of the possibility that distrust and blame-pinning will not be eradicated easily from interaction between sub-populations in our secondary schools. Many factors conspire to reinforce divisions, including the current – and false – devaluation of teachers and the high level of stress. Wise senior management can do much to alleviate this, although the stress of heads and their deputies is deplorably intense. Pastoral heads, in leading their teams of tutors, have an obligation to tackle the stress, and a duty to struggle to overcome these divisive forces. Their role requires them to think more deeply and hold a wider concept of the affective foundations of education. In no sense is the foregoing an argument for preserving the appearance of harmony at all costs, neither does it reify concordance into a self-justifying end. He who waits for consensus before initiating change will still be waiting at doomsday! My intention is to encourage pastoral heads to think and debate, rather than perpetuate the situation where pastoral care in some schools is a bad case of loose concepts.

There are many limitations in the book. Exercises which encourage thoughtful problem-solving play an important part: they do not, however, set a destination; they merely launch pastoral heads on their own path to seeking further knowledge and skill. See them as points of departure for your own adventures in staff development. One omission is obvious. Consideration of pastoral heads' role and skills in dealing with pupils who have special needs, eg withdrawn pupils, those showing anxiety and signs of maladjustment, or experiencing adverse family conditions, has been set aside deliberately. In 1974 I introduced the *active model* of counselling in which the counsellor was a mobiliser of resources, and counselling a joint enterprise involving teachers and pupils. These matters will be dealt with in the second edition of that book, which reflects the development of the active model over the years.

I am aware that many pastoral heads are apprehensive about the future, feeling that the National Curriculum is at odds with the notion of pastoral work. I believe this is misguided: a portrayal of the fact that they are tied to out-of-date notions of pastoral care as an after-the-event form of emotional first aid or as an inferior welfare system. If this were the case, pastoral work would be a drag on the system and an unnecessary brake on progress. Indeed I would lead the movement to sweep it away. Pastoral heads should welcome the challenge of the new initiatives in education as an opportunity to escape from a passive or reactive position. The National Curriculum offers an opportunity to show the relevance of pastoral work to achievement, initiative and responsible socialisation for an exciting technological society. Elsewhere (Hamblin, 1986) I have argued that one of the tasks of pastoral work is to help to equip young people to question with probity the credentials of alleged experts in a technological society. Pupils must be given the skills, not only for successful adaptation to change, but for assessing constructively, and then challenging, forces which erode freedom and dignity. Pastoral work should also make the benefits of the National Curriculum available to all pupils through building individuals' learning styles and encouraging the development of competent learning strategies. Protest about the shortage of resources to undertake the task is crucial. The unending escalation of demands without compensatory support wears down even the most committed teacher. This situation cannot be endured.

But let there be no doubt: pastoral heads must exemplify the principle that as a profession, teachers have the right and duty to fight for the ideal of the school as a caring community in a world where disjunctions, often unpredictable change and consequent insecurity may well be the norm. To play their part with integrity, pastoral heads urgently need to extend their skills. Equally important is their need to abjure the blame-pinning and negativism they are striving to eliminate in the school.

1 The context and nature of staff development in pastoral care

The rationale

This book applies counselling values and skills to the problems of staff development in pastoral care. Values must inform skills: without them, skills become blunt weapons, two-edged swords, or create the impression of development without any fundamental change taking place. Principles are therefore fundamental. As guides to sound action they protect both the helper and the helped, although they can be used manipulatively to justify things which should not be endured. Below are the counselling values which should permeate staff development.

1 The counsellor never removes the responsibility from those with whom he or she works. They are expected to make constructive rational decisions after careful exploration of the problem *in its context*.
2 The counsellor and his or her clients face the facts as squarely and honestly as possible once they have emerged. Pre-categorisations of people and events have to be avoided, whilst the need for clarification of the significance of situations is seen as essential.
3 Counsellors therefore strive to look at problems from the perspectives of those involved, using their own experiences to illuminate, without imposing their views of what the problem *ought* to be about.
4 Interaction in counselling is imbedded in the mutual respect and responsibility which emerge as the process deepens. Trust has to be earned, and credibility is not seen as automatically stemming from the occupation of a senior position.

These principles suggest that staff development in pastoral care is a tentative process based on negotiation. They also highlight the fact that there is no single right way, accepting that what works in one school will not necessarily work in another.

Teacher stress

Facing the facts begins with recognition of the realities of teacher stress. Unhappy and stressed teachers are likely to interpret staff development as an unjustified imposition. Teachers are committed to the well-being of pupils, wishing to do things well, yet this is an age in which they are devalued, many factors eroding the job satisfaction to which they are entitled. Stress is high, as Kyriacou and Sutcliffe (1978), Dunham (1984) and Kyriacou (1986) have shown. Dobson (1982) refers to the 'burnout syndrome' in American teachers which is the equivalent of battle fatigue. The symptoms are exhaustion, sleeplessness, loss of interest in work, depression, hypertension and other related physiological conditions. He cites the International Labour Organization's claim that battle fatigue is found in around a quarter of the teaching profession in the USA, Sweden and Britain. The percentage in the secondary sector is probably higher than this overall figure.

D'Arienzo et al (1982) and Morgan (1983) found evidence of stress amongst teachers responsible for pupils with special needs. The latter produced some evidence that the teachers studied believed that teaching had become a multi-faceted profession, and therefore inherently more stressful. Dobson's observation that we are trapped by stereotypes of teachers which operated in the nineteenth and early twentieth centuries when teaching was not seen as stressful is relevant. Tensions are created by these conflicting pictures of teaching. This culture lag is more marked in the general public, but exists within the profession. Defensive statements, such as 'I didn't come into teaching to do this' and 'I'm paid to teach' have idiosyncratic functions for their users, but are also evidence of psychological and social strains created by the wider views of teaching for which some of us are unready. Failure of parents, politicians and the community to acknowledge the stress inherent in teaching increases the insecurity and vulnerability of teachers. Conscientious and over-stretched teachers are hard put to cope constructively with the view held by sections of the public that teaching is an easy task, and teachers are self-indulgent creatures telling pupils to do what they do not do themselves.

Staff development has to take this context into account. Emphasis on evaluation and appraisal in a climate where teachers feel attacked, and their difficulties ignored, stimulates defences such as displaced aggression, of which the developer becomes the focus. Dunham remarked on the tendency of some male teachers under stress to cope by resort to grim 'gallows' humour. In cases I have observed this insulates them against the worst impact of stress, but destroys their capacity to relate to, and meet, the needs of others, putting them into extreme positions from which they cannot withdraw without unacceptable loss of face.

Teachers wear themselves out in an unending struggle against apathy, passive aggression, evasiveness and minimal performance characterised by imprecise – sometimes inconsistent – attempts to motivate pupils. Profligate unfocused use of energy which is the response to the intense demands of daily life in school leaves them on their knees at the end of the term watching pupils who have been untouched by the process whirling like dervishes; or so it seems to the exhausted teacher. The argument is simple: if there are processes operating among pupils which restrict their performance, making our hard work as teachers less effective and reducing *our* rewards, then it is sensible to do something about it because our pupils' achievement confirms our own professional competence. These processes act largely independently of teaching methods and curriculum content as part of the hidden agenda of the school.

Conscientiousness is still the hallmark of teachers: they set themselves severe and stretching targets; whilst their strongest concern is that shortage of time and resources prevent them from living up to their professional standards. Feeling like this, they then meet constant messages that yesterday's performances and competencies are not good enough for today. The already stressed teacher then feels that the security stemming from the past has been lost. Industry knows the danger of this. Ballinger (1984) citing a study of seven firms noted for their management development, innovation and efficiency, reported that they valued the identity stemming from tradition, and a sense of continuity, using 'anchor men' to maintain them, but flexible responses to change were also encouraged. Teachers faced by current innovations sometimes feel that the past is devalued and suffer a consequent diminution of professional identity. Such clumsy insensitivity by innovators reprehensibly ignores the fact that the old and the new when engaged in constructive interaction produce organic development. Staff development stumbles, distorts or fails when it does not take into account the dominant values and patterns of behaviour in the school which have their roots in the past. Beliefs about the nature of discipline, or what certain groups of pupils can, and should, learn, are essential parts of the context for staff development in which historical elements play a significant part. Meaning only emerges when a keen 'historical' eye scans the situation. Lieberman and Miller (1979) argue strongly that staff development has been targeted too exclusively on personal change. Insufficient attention is paid to organisational influences, or ensuring that organisational structures are capable of adapting to the intended changes in individuals. Team work and group problem solving is essential, but first we must understand what is happening within different groups.

Handy and Aitken (1986) discussing the school as an organisation, give prominence to the need for a common purpose and set of beliefs. This proper emphasis has to be accompanied by a critical approach – is it merely a ceremonial device for maintaining a public image? Those responsible for staff development have to take into account some aspects of Mannheim's (1936; 1956) sociology of knowledge. At the risk of over-simplification, I see Mannheim as implicitly distinguishing between the *truth of propositions* and *truth as the individual's response to reality*. The latter suggests that our picture of the world varies with the different frames of reference provided by the significant sub-cultures to which we belong. Put starkly, it is risky to implement staff development without taking into account the proposition derived from Mannheim that perceptions of truth are, at least partially, dependent on one's position in a social structure. Evaluations undertaken by pastoral and deputy heads in 40 schools are summarised below. I acknowledge that the summary does scant justice to the high quality of the material, which generally reflected the professional honesty and commitment of those undertaking the arduous task. I appreciate their efforts, and have deep respect for their sincerity. Following the Mannheimian position the basic assumption was that pastoral care might well mean different things to different individuals: the meanings varying with their holder's position and status in the school. This is a useful reminder that while the contemporary emphasis on teachers' own definitions of their needs as the framework for their training and development is potentially constructive, we also need to appreciate what is shaping their perceptions, bearing in mind the possibility that hidden constraints are at work. Teachers' initial self-formulations of needs may be partial or biased. The prime element may be stimulating self-awareness which is then followed by negotiation. This recognition of the need for clarification, highlighted earlier as fundamental to counselling, reveals the limitations of training *per se*, and the importance of an open-ended concept of growth which could take forms unanticipated at the commencement of the developmental project.

Evaluations of the type to be summarised obviously have fullest meaning in the context of a particular school: strengths, tensions, cohesiveness and divisions then appear. Each evaluator was able to gain a clear idea of the factors which would facilitate or block development in his or her school. It is the general trends and problems which will be considered here, alerting readers who wish to innovate and encourage staff development.

Evaluators conducted identical interviews with the different sub-populations of their school. Asking the same questions in the same order with minimal intervention from the interviewer allowed reasonable comparability. The sub-populations studied were senior management, heads of academic departments, pastoral heads and classroom teachers. Pupils' views were not solicited, but Hamblin (1984) reports briefly on pupils' perceptions of pastoral care in 55 schools.

Evaluators compared and briefly summarised the concordance and disagreement between the viewpoints of:

- senior management and heads of year or house;
- senior management and classroom teachers;
- heads of academic departments and heads of year or house;
- heads of year or house and classroom teachers.

Nine questions, stemming from discussion with a number of teachers occupying different positions in schools, were used in the interviews.

1 What do you see as the objectives of pastoral care in this school?
2 In what ways could pastoral care in this school be improved?
3 What do you think is the relationship between pastoral work and the curriculum in this school?
4 In what ways, if any, would you like to change the relationship between the pastoral and curricular?

5 What difficulties reduce the effectiveness of tutor work in this school?
6 What needs for training of:
   a) heads of year or house;
   b) form tutors;
   do you see as important?
7 Why do you think teachers sometimes reject tutorial activity?
8 Comment briefly on the frustrations met in pastoral work, suggesting ways in which they could be rectified.
9 In which ways do you think pastoral activity will develop in the future?

These questions reflect issues which seemed salient to teachers attending courses on pastoral care, touching on problems which worried them. General themes emerged, forming the background to more specific points of particular significance to each school. The need for time was uppermost in every sub-population. There was no evidence whether this source of frustration could be overcome by reallocation of time from other activities or by better use of existing time for registration or assemblies. Certain staffs regarded it as a constraint incapable of resolution: sometimes as a feature of professional life providing a convenient target for aggressive complaint; or as offering an excuse for inaction to those seeking one. Developers seeking credibility should begin by breaking into the problem of lack of time. Senior management will have to look for strategies for creating slack, for example, a head of year and pupils taking a long assembly for another year group, setting the head of year free to work with tutors. Such measures are insufficient in themselves, however; they need to be backed by INSET days and other devices such as early closures. Parent education and support will be essential. Let me make my position clear. Teachers cannot allow themselves to be trapped in a situation of ever-increasing demands on their time: this erodes efficiency. Staff development is a proper professional activity; as such it should be conducted within official working hours, either through early or partial closure of the school, the allocation of training days at the beginning of each term – with follow-up and feedback during the term – or a version of the 'continental day' in which teachers have no pressures to undertake lunch duties. Afternoons are then set aside for preparation, marking, training, and staff development. I do not underestimate the difficulties – as a profession we should fight for the facilities.

Hearteningly, the need for in-service training was recognised and endorsed by every group. Interesting discrepancies existed: in one school classroom teachers saw a strong need for pastoral heads to receive training, but the heads of year seemed unaware of their colleagues' perceptions and were apparently satisfied with their current skills.

Many heads of academic departments and class teachers were uncertain of the value of tutorial work, questioning whether it aided pupils' progress. The overall bias, however, was towards uncertainty rather than hostility. Tutorial activity was felt to be outside their training and skill: doubt and lack of knowledge were the salient factors. The need for staff development was clear in the comments. Stress, anxiety and lack of recognition permeate these evaluations, often leaving the impression that no-one knew how to change the situation.

Senior management views
Senior management seemed to agree that:

1 Pastoral care is about the development of the individual.
2 A major function is the support it should give to the learning process: by implication, therefore, the integration of the pastoral and curricular is seen as desirable.
3 The role of the form tutor should be extended and strengthened.
4 Inservice training for both pastoral heads and form tutors is essential.
5 Counselling skills were strongly endorsed as a key element of training. (Note that the evaluations provide no evidence as to what is meant by counselling.)
6 'Pastoral activity in the form it had taken in the 70s was irrelevant, eg pastoral activity in the 1970s sense is a "dead letter" and new definitions are needed.'

These general trends went hand in hand with striking differences between schools, and divisiveness within the senior management of a school. Stands had been taken up; territory established and demarcated; and confusions abounded. The way in which pastoral effort becomes conflict-ridden even in a good school is well illustrated in this excerpt:

The head recognises that too often pastoral work is a mopping up process which is often left to a minority in many cases. They feel there is a need to develop the system of pastoral care but are unsure of how to go about it. ... recognises that pastoral care won't develop unless we have in-service training, but is unable to play an active part in that process. The most able member of the team is ... who feels frustrated at her lack of involvement and almost 'total exclusion from the pastoral side of things' ... The feelings and desires seem to be right, but there is a lack of impetus from ... and a feeling of impotence from ... with regard to the integration of the pastoral and curricular. At the moment it appears to be creating a 'stalling' effect in the present organisation.

In a few schools senior management saw pastoral work almost exclusively in terms of tension management or coping with immediate problems, for example

There was little or no insight into or awareness of the practical, developmental aspects of pastoral care. 'Form tutors were likely to know the children best', (although form tutor contact time consists of five minutes registration morning and afternoon; any class contact being coincidental), and 'should be able to spot any problems' ... the other senior administrative staff felt form tutor training to be a matter of 'guidance such as that offered to a probationary teacher' in affairs of day-to-day administration.

The uncertainties of senior management reflected below will preoccupy those responsible for staff development:

They were aware of the difficulties affecting the success of pastoral care: lack of time for Year Heads and Form Tutors; overlarge tutor-groups; lapses in communication; the unsuitability of some form tutors for the work involved. Not all were certain about the value of time-tabling as a means of combating the first two difficulties, and none was sure of the answers to the second two.

Tensions arose for senior management from the unwillingness of established teachers to learn new skills or adopt new approaches. Some recognised that despite their more informed views, staff generally saw pastoral care as a limited form of discipline, or as a device for dealing with routine administration. Occasionally, they cited the resistance or disinclination of pupils as a barrier to pastoral progress.

A counselling approach, for example that of Perls (1965; 1969), helps people discover how they defeat themselves. One self-defeating situation, given below, may indicate lack of planning and evaluation:

Lack of overall planning associated with 'preoccupation of key personnel with the wrong level of intervention, eg Head of School expected to undertake Head of Year's tasks; Heads of Year undertake Form Tutors' work therefore Form Tutors feel underused and of diminished value.

Frustration was expressed by senior management about 'Inconsistency between houses' which created apparently intractable problems for senior management, and the fact that 'Pastoral problems arise from disaffection with the curriculum'. Forces may be at work restraining senior management from being active change agents. Developers must understand this, rather than joining in the blame-pinning which permeates the secondary school. Buckley (1985) shows the tensions arising from heads having to cope with a present saturated with problems and a future dominated by uncertainties. This 'present/future dilemma' permeates the senior management team and exhausts them. Developers who ignore this reality are in danger of collusion with staff who use the senior management as scapegoats. It is an open question as to what underlies the recording of the laudable aims of senior management ending with, 'However, these emerge as a mere expression of hopes, rather than a determination to achieve this'.

The views of pastoral heads
Pastoral heads shared the endorsement of the need for tutors to take more responsibility and enlarge their sphere of activity. Their general orientation inclined towards the pessimistic, focusing on the lack of tangible results for their efforts, the inability of tutors to see any benefits from tutor work, and the perplexing task of convincing others of the importance of tutor work. Examples of the attitudes of ineffectiveness that developers will have to challenge are:

The historical divide between curriculum and pastoral care was still evident, and from some colleagues there was an in-built resistance to change.

A more pessimistic view of pastoral care in the school was apparent ..., the feeling being that they lacked esteem amongst colleagues partly because of relatively low status in terms of salary and rank – it is a 'pastoral system on the cheap'.

Frustrations mentioned included role conflict 'between being a listener and a chastiser' and 'Trying to balance discipline with a caring role'.

The final extract is enlightening: it suggests that pastoral heads have to question the dichotomies of this type. Failure to resolve them can trap pastoral heads into inconsistent actions; arousing emotional tensions and feelings of inadequacy. Some may not even be aware of such tensions. They may be the small group who saw no need for training for themselves or for tutors, such as the person who stated: 'I've been married and brought up my own children!'; a statement which evinces a total lack of awareness of the contributions to curriculum development and learning now expected from pastoral heads. The latent image is one of benevolent maternalism or paternalism, of which the pupil is to be the passive recipient. The majority saw training as a precondition for development.

The link between the pastoral and curricular was seen as a two-way process, not confined to pastoral support of the teaching methods. Improvement of pastoral care depended on a better curriculum and change of classroom methods, for example:

More attention should be paid to the curriculum – strong feeling that some of the discipline problems may be solved by offering a better 'diet' particularly to the less able.

Divisions between pastoral and curricular responsibilities artificial – often pastoral problems are result of curriculum ineffectiveness or inappropriateness, therefore need resolving at source not symptom.

Closer contact between pastoral and academic heads was seen as desirable. Developers need to facilitate situations in which pastoral and academic heads work in tandem, leading tutor teams in problem-solving and training. In three cases pastoral heads would welcome the return of at least some disciplinary functions to academic heads:

Improvements: Returning disciplinary functions to Heads of Department.

More democracy needed: HODs help with discipline, pastoral heads advise on curriculum.

The ways in which these interchanges would be achieved were not spelt out, but the excerpts reflect the desire of many pastoral heads to bridge, or at least narrow, the pastoral–curricular divide. Concern was expressed about poor communication, whilst in other schools doubt was voiced about the heavy expenditure of time on a few pupils without commensurate results. The statement below touches on sources of difficulty:

> ... time and the demands of administration. Tutors not feeling the whole experience of pupils in their group is their responsibility. Staff find it difficult to change roles, subject orientated, lack of willingness to train, easily discouraged when pupil is not immediately 'keen'. Lack of negotiation between tutor and tutor group about pastoral curriculum.

Signals for developers are clear in the rigid perceptions of 'find it difficult to change roles' and the 'lack of negotiation between tutor and tutor group about pastoral curriculum' which denies pupils involvement in, and a sense of ownership of, the pastoral programme. Some pastoral heads saw few, if any, links between the pastoral and curricular. In one school, the evaluator reported that they 'gasped at the question!'. Some focused on a negative relationship, viz problems for the pastoral team were generated by poorly taught or inappropriate curricula, therefore the developer cannot ignore Buckley's (1980) point that efficient teaching is effective pastoral care.

The viewpoints of academic heads
Hamblin (1977) writing on 'The Pastoral Team: Illusion or Reality?', draws attention to the pervasiveness of role conflict. Occupation of multiple roles created conflict for pastoral heads, but role conflict is just as significant for the academic heads. Conflicts between tutor work and their other duties were obvious in their reported views. Yet they generally felt that the responsibilities of tutors should be increased, some including increased parental contact. Their main concern was for the progress of students within their subjects, but they were alert to the value of pastoral care in helping to ensure this. Caution about over-involvement personally in pastoral roles did not prevent endorsement of the value of backup provided by year heads, eg 'sources of strength lay in their liaison with year heads'. Other evaluators reported that:

> Heads of department have an incomplete view of pastoral care: they recognise their lack of expertise and consider the best thing is to leave it alone.

This reference to lack of knowledge is echoed in this statement:

> Too many assumptions are made as to what tutors know ... More people were becoming aware of children's problems but lack of knowledge as to how to deal with them was reducing the prestige of pastoral care.

The importance of understanding the views of each sub-population is clear: departmental heads accepted their need to learn more about pastoral care, but felt that heads of year or house devalue the curriculum, and that they in turn 'should keep up with curriculum'.

The excerpts below alert developers to the wide range of tensions they could face:

> There was a general resentment about the position of Heads of Year who appear to have more autonomy than themselves ... About 25% of Heads of Department showed a genuine interest in the pastoral affairs of the school and saw their role as form tutor as being an important one which they would like to develop.

> Interest in pastoral care 'new' and threatening to their share of resources in all senses. They feel the school 'worked' before this further structure was added. They see Year Heads as an alternative power structure especially when Year Heads attend departmental meetings re options etc.

> All desire a greater integration between the pastoral and the curricular but feel the link is tenuous at the moment. ... A desire to play a more active part in the pastoral process and to make their role more meaingful, 'If HOD are to help more, there needs to be more of a balance' ... I feel the underlying tensions are those of:
>   *Resentment* of what they feel is their exclusion from the pastoral role.
>   *Frustration* with their own role definition (or lack of it) and a certain sense of powerlessness.
>   *Jealousy* (limited) of the perceived status of HOY, and of practical points such as amount of free time, availability of office and telephone.

... A dissatisfaction with the way in which their roles are functioning, but a good consensus of opinion with regard to the way in which pastoral care should operate. There also appears to be a feeling for a new direction ...

The views of class teachers

Whilst far from totally negative, it was clear that significant numbers of class teachers were suspicious, and therefore likely to resist any extension of their work. Tinges of the pastoral–curricular divide are present in the statement below, yet it is not unreasonable; development demands that such issues should be tackled.

> Tutors are busy, hard-working and subject-based, and subject's success is more easily evaluated. How will pastoral care be evaluated? ... Some tutors were already 'refusing' to use tutor group activity before it had been explained fully to them.

Role conflicts abounded, for example:

> The major function reducing effectiveness was felt to be the conflict between roles as a teacher/disciplinarian and as a form tutor. Contact with tutees is often of a negative, punitive nature. The children regarded tutorial work as an intrusion on their time.

Many points arise for developers in this: the concept of discipline seems to be negative, and equated with punishment; the students' concept of 'their time' is equally interesting. In reading similar comments one felt they showed teachers under stress who had the strongly-held impression that senior management had little idea of the weight of pressures on the class teacher. It was noteworthy that groups of teachers acknowledged, albeit sometimes grudgingly, their need for training, but they were usually clear that pastoral heads needed it equally urgently. The full importance of understanding the views of truth held by the sub-groups within the school should now be clearer. The gamut of perceptions and reactions is bewilderingly large: the developers have to assess for themselves what is happening. In the 40 schools investigated, some class teachers voiced their desire for support which they felt was denied them: even more disturbingly, they voiced suspicions that senior management were uncommitted despite their public statements. A sense of grievance almost stereo-typical in nature appeared:

Resentment against teachers using pastoral care as a channel for promotion – some said the less academic progressed that way. Felt some recent developments were 'band-wagon'.

Misunderstanding, lack of confidence in new methods, feeling inadequate, lack of training, activities not always seen as relevant, 'other things' crowd out tutorial work.

Tutors want to be released from their disciplinary function and being the chasers of homework.

Pastoral heads are reproached for incompetent public relationships, insensitivity and poor management, eg 'Teachers often resent being presented with pastoral documents which state the obvious. This is counter-productive as many staff are more than happy to develop pastoral care'.

These statements, with others, touch on fears that pastoral demands will breach the threshold of stress and commitment. Frustrations also came from pupils' resistance, their limited views of the purpose of school, and the difficulty of evaluating their interest in pastoral activity. Some evidence suggests that pastoral heads have few ideas about how to gain greater credibility, and are insensitive to the anxieties of class teachers, labelling them as 'resistant'. Lack of team work and support create sterility, exacerbating difficulties. The extreme position is illustrated in this excerpt:

Much criticism of the pettiness of HoYs – in some cases seeming to create jobs for the sake of it – bad PR job. . . . Majority of form tutors feel they are undermined in their efforts, eg lack of information; not asked to participate in dealings with pupils and/or parents.

The young teacher may be more flexible in approach, although there is little evidence that age or subject are important factors. One evaluator specifically mentions age and experience:

The youngest and least experienced were in general enthusiastic about the possibilities of pastoral care and felt the school had a duty to educate the whole child. They saw the form tutor as important and enjoyed the challenge this presented . . . [Underlining not in the original]

The young teacher's co-operation should not, however, be taken for granted: the legacy of inadequate tutor work is already in schools; in a recent training day I met two probationary teachers holding negative attitudes towards pastoral activity because of ill-judged and puerile experiences they had endured at school. Recalling their marginal position in the profession, it is significant that they remained obdurate in the face of senior management persuasions.

The fear of many teachers when pastoral demands are couched imprecisely is that acquiescence means entering a situation of ever-increasing activity where the threshold for stress will be breached and their capacity for commitment outstripped. Counselling approaches sensitise developers to the way in which our perceptions play an important part in shaping our behaviour, and how our assumptions shape those perceptions. Fear of failure, revelation of inadequacy or the violation of beliefs about the proper social distance between teacher and student have to be taken into account as possible explanations of hostility or unwillingness.

Comparison of senior management and pastoral heads'
viewpoints

Discrepancies were apparent between the two groups' views of the nature and purposes of pastoral care and what is happening within the school. In extreme cases, confusions contribute to profound misunderstandings which could be used to justify existing conflict. In one school, management seemed to see things as satisfactory, but pastoral heads felt they were barely containing endemic crisis. In another, senior management saw pastoral heads as unimaginative, resisting necessary change, whilst the pastoral heads felt they were unsupported and being asked to cope with over-rapid change. The result was 'buck passing' on both sides. The picture held by one group of the other is critical in shaping interaction; 'The majority of SM team communicated a lack of confidence in Heads of House: this is perceived quite clearly by HoHs and is resented.' Or the reverse may obtain: 'SM often felt unsupported by HOYs' capricious autonomy'.

Concord about objectives is no guarantee of unanimity about the way of achieving them: 'Contrasts between the realization of that aim: either the disciplinary/authority approach or a caring approach.' Concern is voiced 'that we are re-establishing a system of punitive attrition rather than developing a system of active pastoral care'. Senior management tended to see training as essential for all personnel, but pastoral heads stressed it as necessary for tutors, ignoring their own needs.

Such discordances feed unprofitable conflict: yet my experience suggests they are left untouched by current training. Even the positive views of senior management are sometimes ignored; 'Heads of year see their role as more mundane and status lower than senior management would like.'

Comparison of senior management and class teachers' views

Senior management have the wider view of development. Class teachers see time and personal involvement as critical: their viewpoints carry an urgency absent in those of senior management and simultaneous pessimism about the outcomes of change. They were more conscious of immediately pressing problems, certainly more ready to express them:

> Senior management's ambitions seem to be class teachers' fears.

> Senior management equals a 'theoretical' approach. Classroom teachers concerned with 'practical' survival.

Divergences appear clearly in this statement:

> Classroom teachers feel that the strongest discouraging factor in pastoral work is the *clash* between role as a teacher/ disciplinarian and as a form tutor, whereas senior staff felt it was lack of adequate training and/or experience. Classroom teachers often more concerned with the individual and his/her progress. Senior management seem more system orientated.

The stark description below illustrates the folly of rushing into staff development without assessing the tensions. Schools in such a situation as this destroy the unthinking innovator who becomes the target for displaced aggression:

> Management and teachers don't trust one another and fears of conspiracies abound. Management often under-rate staff good-will and commitment because they fear a few strong individuals who will stand up for themselves. Staff fear that management will lump more work on them, and opt out.

Superficial consensus about the objectives of education and the goals of the school can hide a devious hidden agenda in which such alienation between groups, although masked by good manners, produces barren interaction which exhausts all concerned. Agreement on the point of change does not eradicate deep misconceptions as the following illustrates:

> ... both groups saw the tutor as the focal point of the system. Tutors expressed many personal difficulties and frustrations about things perceived as beyond their control whereas S thought tutors' own awareness and view of the tasks was highly relevant and could improve matters.

Contrasting views of academic and pastoral middle management
The legacy of the expediency in which pastoral work was rooted is the separation of the pastoral and curricular. Pastoral and academic heads must work closely and supportively together if pastoral care is to support the subject teaching (Marland, 1974), and help develop active learning through teaching problem-solving and decision-making skills. Learning has to become an active debate not only between teacher and pupil, but between pupil and pupil (Hamblin, 1978, 1981, 1986). Co-operation will be far from easy, but the reasons do not lie in the alleged obduracy of academic heads – so often put forward as explanation by pastoral heads. Both groups are responsible for the pastoral-curricular divide. Some departmental heads felt year heads usurped their functions; others saw pastoral care as a half-hearted attempt to solve pupils' problems; heads of year felt they could give better service if they did not have to spend so much time dealing with pupils' poor work. Mutual blaming creates a situation of stalemate, allowing both parties to pursue a subdued conflict with good consciences, a situation exemplified below:

> Main complaint of HOD is that no attempt is made by HOY to involve them in the pastoral structure in a significant way. HOY point out that HOD are often disparaging with regard to pastoral aspects, and are purely concerned with the academic work of their own departments.

Pastoral heads *assumed* that departmental heads were indifferent, probably antagonistic to pastoral work (including their role as a form tutor) when in fact they appreciated the importance of pastoral work. A role conflict existed for some, however: they felt that if they did all they ought to do as a tutor they would be in danger of becoming inefficient as departmental heads. Pressures and rigidities apparently existed which prevented pastoral heads from registering and empathising with colleagues' dilemmas. Be clear that acknowledging the worth of pastoral care does not necessarily mean backing current organisational forms. In my developmental work I have met academic heads who would like to develop pastoral work within their subject department, integrating the pastoral and curricular productively – certainly providing the opportunity for pastoral and academic heads to work in tandem. Questions of territory might arise; but this would be better than the school investigated by Doherty (1981) where academic heads saw pastoral care as a limited subservient activity to be tolerated for its convenience value, and pastoral heads as their handmaids.

Misperceptions seem endemic, but if apprehended, they can be corrected. Even the simple methods used in these evaluations brought conflicts into the open, rendering them capable of resolution, as the following example illustrates.

> (The year heads) felt they were offering as much guidance as they could as far as materials, approaches, etc were concerned – and that often, such guidance was being rejected – whereas the heads of department felt the tutor work was not well organised and that insufficient guidance was being given which was leading to confusion and rejection of tutorial work.

Undoubtedly strong emotions will be evoked, and the developers need the skills of managing conflict. Evasion of professional debate on such tensions as those above, or denial of their existence for the sake of retaining the semblance of solidarity, is almost certainly collusion – the maintenance of a deceptive definition of reality – with ineffectiveness. Sensitive adaptations would be essential in these situations:

> HOYs very open, although defensive when pushed. Some HODs, although agreeing in public, have deep reservations about pastoral care. HODs see HOYs as failed HODs. Both groups for different reasons wanted discipline back with HODs. HODs are aware of losing ground in the power structure in the last few years.

> Both desire a more effective pastoral care system, but considered from different perspectives. Each group unaware of the real feelings and perceptions of the other.

Viewpoints of pastoral heads and class teachers
Blame-pinning is more determined by emotive forces than rational assessment in many cases. One wonders which was more influential in class teachers' 'perception that Year Heads want to be liked rather than enforce discipline'. Class teachers sometimes felt that pastoral care meant judgement of them, and not of pupils – a finding akin to that reported in Hamblin (1984) where form tutors felt blamed for the misdeeds of their forms. Discrepancies were reported which must rebound on pupils:

> HOYs see objectives as fulfilling school aims, classroom teachers see it as a discipline function only.

> Class teachers deeply frustrated over the lack of respect shown to them by HOY and frustrated over the lack of pertinent and meaningful advice and information.

Evasive mechanisms are described, operating as a form of passive or indirect aggression, probably reflecting a malaise that pervaded the value climate of the school:

> Both groups tended to pass responsibility upwards in the hier-archy – negative collaboration. Collective feeling of being unappreciated; constructive efforts not rewarded, eg suggestions not acted on or fully discussed, feeling of discouragement.

Such factors are not peculiar to pastoral care; the greater legitimacy of curricular activity does not exempt it from them, but ours is a limited concern. Until they are tackled there will be no end to unproductive tensions. Let one evaluator speak:

> There is a lot of disillusionment here caused by the confusion of roles. The heads of year are totally untrained at leading or training. They have no idea what their role is or where the year is going. They plan programmes which are never implemented as the difficulties of classroom teachers are not faced. The heads of year lack the expertise to analyse and help willing teachers. Therefore there are endless meetings and discussions which come to naught.

Risks are involved in tackling these problems, but awareness, coupled with anticipation within the ethos of counselling, provide us with the opportunity to modify and rebuild, rather than remaining victims of unthinking routines.

The nature of staff development for pastoral care

The counselling process helps individuals change their attitudes and behaviours so that they yield more satisfaction to themselves and others in their life space. This is also what staff development is about. It is possible to misinterpret the situation as one of unilateral influence where one person operates as a change agent causing the other to react. But we have seen that counselling reinforces the responsibility of people, striving to ensure they make choices knowingly and changes purposefully. De Charms (1968) distinguishes between pawns who are at the mercy of forces outside their control and those who determine the goals they wish to achieve. Staff development boosts colleagues' capacity for determining goals, and consequently their sense of ownership of them.

My simple definition includes the word 'change', but there is no assumption that all changes are equally valuable, or that the more change there is the better things will be. Over-rapid change may be detrimental even if staff are willingly involved. Enthusiasm generated by the novelty effect cannot be maintained indefinitely. Emotional adjustments can be neglected in a wave of innovatory zeal, and then participants are overwhelmed by self-doubt when unanticipated frustrations appear. Smith (1976) reporting on learning to learn in adult education comments on the generation of relatively intense feelings when personal change is required. It may be tempting to gloss over the emotive aspects of staff development, but the cost can be a superficial appearance of change unrooted in internal adjustments. All of us find it hard – perhaps bitter – to discard long-held frameworks of judgement and action; the loss of the associated justifications leaves us feeling naked. We tote around implicit personality theories about others' motivation and the reasons for their behaviour which shape our judgements and reactions unknown to us. Exposing and challenging these built-in assumptions forms the groundwork of staff development. It is all too easy for trainers to make loose dispositional inferences about a colleague's remarks, assuming them to be significant indicators of hostility or resistance when they may be a product of antecedent conditions: frustration stemming from a classroom incident or an unrelated clash with a colleague.

Good staff development brings awareness that honestly held differences in judgements have to be explored. After a clash or a crisis, the people involved interpret their behaviour in terms of their knowledge of themselves and their past experience. An observer of the incident will explain it on the basis of his or her beliefs about how others would behave in those circumstances – a broad comparison process is at work. There is a potentially dangerous twist in this. Jones and Nisbett (1972) follow up the original work of Bruner and Taguiri (1954), pointing out the different perspectives of actors and observers. The former blame the situation or centre sharply on it in explaining their actions, whilst the latter usually concentrate on relating the behaviour to the actors' personalities, seeing it as evidence of temperament or character. Topping (1983) and Coulby and Harper (1985) show the limitations and handicaps we fabricate by paying attention solely to the personality of the disruptive pupil rather than giving due account to the situation in which the behaviour occurs. It would be perverse to discard this self-defeating behaviour in dealing with pupils, yet retain it in staff development. Suspension of immediate crude judgements which automatically invoke personality is essential if staff development is to incorporate sensitively guided continuous reflection.

Let there be no illusion about the difficulty of staff development in pastoral care. Stress, and the closed views of the sub-groups, are added to by Griffin's (1983) argument that teachers at 'modest conceptual stages' will have difficulty in comprehending why counselling skills should be used in teaching. They may well find it as difficult to accept them as the framework for development in pastoral care, although the conditions outlined earlier make them imperative.

Griffin sees staff development as any systematic effort intended to change the professional behaviours, beliefs and understanding of teachers which leads towards an articulated end. Bradley *et al* (1983) cite Piper and Glatter (1977) whose approach echoes the 'systematic' emphasis and also asserts the importance of constructively relating the individuals' interests and 'their carefully assessed requirements' for career development to the future development of the organisation. I would hope the approach in pastoral care would deepen colleagues' capacity to respond to future developments and increase their job satisfaction. If career development means promotion it is more problematical: it may divide rather than integrate; for example, one evaluator reported, 'Resentment against teachers using pastoral care as a channel for promotion – some said the less able progressed that way'. Persistence will be needed to break into the cynicism of staff who see no need for improvement in their work, but they are a minority. Bradley *et al* suggest that some teachers anticipate that the result of staff development will be a list of intended actions and outcomes which are never achieved – it will merely be a matter of 'going through the motions'. But it need not be like that: strengths can be identified and built on; credibility gradually acquired. Consideration of the negative possibilities before initiating the first steps in development is crucial; coping with it is part of the process. We have seen earlier that no longer is the scapegoat confined to the wilderness, for each sub-group in the school resolutely maintains its own. Pastoral development begins by allowing the sub-population perspectives which allocate blame and reject professional responsibility to be acknowledged, analysed and understood. Bradley *et al* give wise advice when they urge developers to understand the institution as a prerequisite for charting paths for development.

The process of staff development

As Lieberman and Miller (1979) insist, we start where people are, not where we want – or I would add, where we imagine – them to be. Behind the earlier material of this chapter is recognition that training in specific skills, whilst necessary, is insufficient for long-lasting change. At the heart of pastoral development is team building. Colleagues then provide mutual support as problems are faced. For example, a team approach to the modification of the attitudes and behaviour of a difficult class relieves stress on colleagues who have felt isolated and that it is *their* problem only, whilst the consistent application of the measures adopted makes success more likely.

Next, the orientation is towards growth rather than fixation on deficits: building on strengths rather than blaming people defensively. Deprivations have to be acknowledged and tackled. Foremost is time. If government, LEAs and others are serious about staff development they must make time available within working hours. (Some movement towards this has already occurred.) Subjects which are timetabled have greater status than those pushed into a marginal position as out-of-school pursuits. Voluntary commitment to training is laudable, yet reliance on it is interpreted as evidence of the low value of the activity by those who need it most. They then escape examination of their practices and exposure to the views of colleagues. Frequently I meet the comment, 'This is the first time we have been able to work as a team!' They have been denied the possibility of developing at a professional level a shared framework or common language which encourages the systematic application of analytic thought to the resolution of the problems which beset them. Some of us then resort to defensive, possibly cynical, reactions as a way of maintaining equilibrium in a situation from which there seems no creative escape. For some, staffroom communication acts as a form of catharsis, but the reduction and control of tension does nothing to change the problems. TVEI, CPVE and other recent developments have helped us overcome our bafflement about the older pupil who saw school as irrelevant and unrewarding because he or she prejudged, predicted failure and defended themselves against change. Yet is not the teacher who, in the face of what seems remorseless change, uses every experience to fuel his or her resistance, taking the 'it won't work' approach or discrediting the committed by dismissing them as 'empire builders' still a colleague worthy of equal consideration? Their views may be justifiable from their position in the school, and condemnation merely makes them cling to their viewpoint more strongly.

Staff development in pastoral work means patience with the irritating teacher who seems to be seeking all-embracing answers to problems – the 'What do I do if . . .'. When told no recipe is available, they react by dismissing the whole thing as rubbish, abdicating their proper professional responsibility for decision-making. This seems to be a facet of the theoretical-practical dichotomy evident in class teachers' perceptions of senior management. Lecturers know that many teachers see them as evading the task of telling the audience what to do to resolve a specific problem. They also know that if they did the response would be, 'It won't work!' These tendencies have to be grappled with rather than ignored.

Resistances of this type are not to be glossed over, but it is warming to recall that TRIST activities revealed a fund of goodwill and initiative. Unco-operativeness can be justifiable in the light of past experience of innovation, as well as being symptomatic of concealed anxiety and inadequacy. A counsellor respects individual differences: expects different rates of development and levels of performance; and certainly does not induce uniformity for its own sake. The developer does the same, using behavioural approaches which encourage people to think about problems in ways which suggest the steps that can be taken to resolve them. Intervention based on the idea of graduation should occur in the areas where results are most likely, breaking into perceptions of the task as impossible.

Teachers I work with tell me that I am talking about the pastoral care of staff. I agree, if pastoral care is seen as a developmental process concerned with mastery and building on strengths, actual and potential.

First, one encourages respect for the importance of the profession and enhancement of a positive picture of the teacher as a professional. A teacher's professional self-concept is deeply influenced by experiences in the probationary year when his or her position in the school and profession is marginal. Evaluations of colleagues and problems of control and organisation can bring insecurity and loss of mastery, causing reliance on a 'survival kit' of a limited type which constrains performance and reduces enthusiasm. Staff development builds what Burns (1982) called self-worth: a positive view of one's basic level of competence and the ability to control the course of one's actions. But professional uncertainty and a sense of being disregarded has been the lot of many of us. How does staff development begin when such feelings are strong?

A down-to-earth start could be based on helping colleagues identify and discuss threatening, stressful and rewarding situations in their pastoral work. Situational self-knowledge builds the sense of competence necessary for professional self-worth. Shared examination of responses to such situations as the provocative pupil stimulate awareness of what underlies routine reactions: less obvious threats, irrational urgings towards fight or flight, feelings of frustration or loss of face and fears of the evaluations of colleagues ... The old principle of psychotherapy that talking in a climate of acceptance reveals the contribution that the individual makes to the events of which he complains is relevant here. But let there be no misinterpretation; the focus is primarily on the professional tasks of the tutor or pastoral head. Insights may be gathered which relate to the inner lives of colleagues. That is a matter for them. The object is to foster professional awareness, not act as an amateur therapist, although the experience itself may be therapeutic.

Pastoral work with pupils should extend their control of their life space, helping them meet the legitimate demands of peers, home and school; staff development does something similar for their teachers. In the secondary school, teaching can be a lonely affair in which one feels compelled to hide real or imagined inadequacies, presenting a carefully manicured image to colleagues. The survival kit adopted as a response to compulsive expectations – the compulsions may be self-generated and perceptions of expectations exaggerated or inaccurate – entails heavy costs for some of us. Some teachers restrict their performance, holding at bay ambiguities, unease and doubt by sharp demarcations about what they do, and the limits of their task. With pupils, we strive to improve peer interaction, provide supports within the group and boost helping relationships. Are we providing the adult professional equivalent for ourselves? If we cared more for one another, we might realise that there are moments for us all when classroom interaction is an unending struggle or battle against indifference which drains us.

Developers taking a counselling approach will have as their ideal the enabling relationship described by Carl Rogers (1961). This is accepting and democratic; based on mutual perceptions of trust and respect, accompanied by responsible independence where staff feel they are making decisions without pressure or obligation. Frequent references to 'the hierarchy' occur in some schools: surely an odd phenomenon in a profession. It is disturbing that such allusions are usually destructively critical, probably indicating that teachers feel harassed, manipulated or constrained by middle and senior management. Misperceptions, or use of 'the hierarchy' to deny professional responsibility for self-evaluation and subsequent action, are undoubtedly present. But staff development should be constructive intervention: there is little point in merely allocating blame; responsible action is needed. Professionals are responsibly autonomous, possessing an expertise which they put at the disposal of their clients whose welfare is prime. Teachers are increasingly meeting these requirements despite shortages of resources, unthinking criticisms by the government and the self-eroding pressures created by dirty schools. Staff development in pastoral care will add to the expertise of teachers. As yet, a third requirement has not been met: control by the profession of entry and surveillance of standards. I hope that day will come. Vigorous striving for enhancement of our skills through programmes of staff development demonstrates our capacity to control our professional destinies. Vigilance is crucial: the evidence from schools given in this chapter reveals misunderstanding between groups, hinting at the ease with which good people become caught up in self-defeating patterns of perception and action. Energy then is diverted into defensive reactions which profit nobody. Courage is needed to break into this situation; yet if our claim of professional status is considered genuine, we must take considered risks. If we care, not only for pupils but for one another, staff development in pastoral work is imperative.

2 Linking the pastoral and curricular

An orientation to pastoral development

The evaluations suggested that truth is anchored to sub-populations, each holding a view of pastoral activity which could conflict with those held by other groups. Where sharp divisions existed between the pastoral and academic, pastoral work seemed condemned to abortive punishment, after-the-event reactions and inferior welfare activity. Hamblin (1984) in evaluating reports from 55 schools, saw the striking neglect of linkage of the pastoral and curricular as an important element of middle management failure. Integration of, or at least, strongly linking, the pastoral and curricular, will contribute to the sense of common purpose stressed by Handy and Aitken (1986) as essential to the school as an effective organisation. It offers the best chance of overcoming the debilitating divisions shown in Chapter One.

Understanding rooted in negotiation, rather than rushing into immediate action, is the soundest foundation for pastoral development. Counselling which insists that problems must be dealt with in the context of the person's whole life has much in common with organisational development as described by Joyce (1983), Lewis (1985) and Schmuck et al (1985). Change in one area of the school usually brings compensatory or complementary change elsewhere. But Cuban's (1984) warning reminds pastoral heads that development is no easy task. Commenting on the all too frequent pattern of enthusiasm followed by frustration and disappointment, he argues that no one knows how to create effective schools. Theories of school improvement are incomplete, and we do not know which approaches, singly or in combination, lead to the desired results. Yet, with professional caution, and avoiding inflated claims, we can stimulate awareness of possible lines of development, and break into the sense that nothing can be done to change things. If the forces operating in the school remain amorphous or mysterious, then pessimism abounds. Joyce *et al* argue that teachers' alienation is closely related to their belief that they are unable to influence their school. Some certainly blame 'the hierarchy' as a way of avoiding self-appraisal and supporting initiatives.

Pastoral heads wanting change have found it useful to:

1 Increase colleagues' alertness to system-based forces which constrain or enhance their performance;
2 Stimulate understanding of the factors underpinning classroom interaction and learning;
3 Help colleagues see that counselling skills applied in the classroom increase co-operation and productivity;
4 Foster appreciation of the benefits of team work in supporting the teacher and increasing job satisfaction.

Such approaches renew sensitivities that have been blunted by an unending battle against apathy and too heavy workloads. They remind us that we need to care for one another as part of caring for pupils.

Yet more is needed than working with the individual. Tackling the disparate group-based versions of truth forces us to look at the school as a whole. Organisational development examines the *whole curriculum* dynamics operating within a particular school. Fullan, Miles and Taylor (1980) describe it as a 'Coherent, systematically planned, sustained effort at system self-study and improvement' – a good description of staff development for pastoral care. Why is a system-based approach essential? Schmuck *et al* claim that a school develops patterns of interaction which are independent of particular individuals: a restatement of the Gestalt view that the whole is more than the sum of its parts. Groups operate in the school which encourage certain orientations to the basic tasks of the school, and, at least implicitly, reward some attitudes and actions, whilst discouraging others, enhancing or reducing the individual's efficiency. These patterns of action then acquire a sense of rightness, and deviation from them brings irrational feelings of being a renegade or deserter. Observation of, and reflection on, such group processes is fundamental to pastoral development.

Pastoral heads have to go beyond the obvious and immediate, and take the riskier step of studying these processes. It is riskier because there is an ever-present danger of misinterpretation or premature imposition of meaning without checking the evidence. The need for this approach is shown if we consider communication. It could be assumed that fuller and clearer communication will resolve difficulties. But analysis of communication between groups – say senior management and classroom teachers – which does not include examination of the attribution of intent to the senders, or the distortions of meaning which occur as directives or documents are discussed in informal groups, and then hardened into shared resistance, is inadequate. Identification of ways in which the upward flow of communication in some schools is modified so that resentments are filtered out, or anxieties denied, is a prerequisite for developing greater trust. These blocks and filters are not deliberate, but have established themselves unnoticed. Much can be done through meetings of the various groups, for example pastoral heads and senior management, year or house heads and their tutors, but the dynamics of those meetings are worthy of study. This occurs in a later chapter. The number of meetings is a source of stress itself, but experience of abortive meetings, or of those which incorporate ritualised interactions confirming established positions or staking out territory, confirms participants' views that change is unnecessary or impossible. Perhaps we have neglected analysis of the basic tools of meetings and discussions. Negotiation is admirable, but I have met teachers who distrust it, seeing it merely as a more pleasant form of coercion or the 'velvet glove', or who cannot enter into it because of their restricted ideas of their role. Criticisms of 'received wisdom' are sometimes valid, but we may be in danger of creating new orthodoxies in which stereotypical prescriptions for more effective meetings are substituted for deeper reflection. In training for staff development it has proved helpful to ask simple *questions* about pastoral meetings, some of which are given below:

1 What were the intended purposes?
2 Did a hidden agenda exist? If so, what was it, and why did it exist?
3 What predictions did participants take into the meeting?
4 Who assumed dominant and passive roles? With what results?

TVEI brought to the forefront the concept of ownership: class teachers often feel that tutorial activities require skills foreign to them, and have no sense that the pastoral programme belongs to them. In pastoral development, colleagues have to be involved in the selection, collection and interpretation of data if it is to be personally relevant and seen as worth acting on. The sense of ownership is acquired at different rates, and pastoral leaders have to adapt to the readiness of their teams. More support needs to be given to some tutors, others need encouragement to go ahead in their own way. Some will need limited and clearly-structured materials, others will view them with distaste as limiting their initiative. Ownership demands adaptation to the needs of individuals, rather than behaving as if individuals in the team are identical. Ownership can be stimulated by simple activities, one of which is outlined below:

> Tutors divide into pairs. Using a simple framework of objectives, core activity and application, they develop a tutor period activity. (See Hamblin, 1984). On completion they then explain their activity to another pair inviting positive suggestions for development. The other pair then repeats the process.

Confidence is given by the shared construction, and ownership strengthened by the exposition.

Counselling skills and leadership styles

Pastoral development is not an experience awash with emotions, but feelings have to be treated with deep respect. I recall with humility the person who said, 'I realise what I need to do differently, and what I could have done but didn't, but do *you* understand what it means to have wasted those years?' Frustration, regret, anger, alienation and exhaustion have to be accepted as part of staff development. The tools used by the pastoral head are those of responsible behavioural counselling (see Krumboltz and Thoresen, 1969; Thoresen and Mahoney, 1974 and Kanfer and Goldstein, 1985) and also cognitive – instructional counselling (see Martin, 1987) together with adaptive counselling as described by Howard *et al* (1987). The behavioural approach helps people look at the problems they have identified in ways which suggest the steps they can take to resolve them. The methods of Martin give the counsellor the role of creative educator who offers opportunities for formulating plans and achieving goals. Martin refers to three groups of counselling skills which can be adapted by the pastoral head in working with a team of tutors:

1 *Soliciting skills*: constructive probing, confronting by calling attention to inconsistencies or obtaining further information.
2 *Reacting skills*: reflecting back meaning and giving encouragement which helps tutors plan.
3 *Structuring skills*: providing summary statements, and demonstrating a way of tackling a problem that stimulates other ideas for its

solution, or providing a list of key questions as a framework for analysis.

The content of each group of skills as given above reflects what I have found important when working with colleagues. It has been useful to hold in mind Martin's distinction between declarative knowledge which explains what is occurring, and procedural knowledge which is rooted in action: the difference between 'knowing that' and 'knowing how'.

Equally important is the work of Howard *et al* (1987) which appears to be developed from the teaching of Hersey and Blanchard (1977) on situational leadership. Adaptive counselling uses the principle that *appropriate management style is determined by the situation, especially the levels of motivation and skill of those they lead*. Reddin (1970) also used in his 3D theory of managerial effectiveness the idea of appropriate situationally-based balances between task orientation and relationship orientation. Hersey and Blanchard see leadership as the 'process of influencing the activities of a person or group in striving for goal achievement in a given situation'. Leadership is a product of interactive relationships between the personality and skills of the leader, the characteristics of followers and relevant features of the situation. Pastoral heads as a group should evaluate and consider this approach. It provides a basis for examining the frequently met difficulty of things being done at the wrong level: senior management doing the work of pastoral heads; the latter doing the work of form tutors.

Nurture and development of the capacities of tutors seem dependent on a balance of supportive and structuring or directive behaviours that are appropriate to a particular group of tutors at a particular phase in the history of the school. Some groups will need more structuring, and others will react negatively to it. There is no universal optimum mix. Argyris (cited in Hersey and Blanchard) argues that there are many pressures which keep people immature *in the organisation*. Anxiety impedes performance, and low confidence activates defensive reactions. Diagnosis of the current situation which looks at the actual state of things, and assesses not only attitudes and relationships, but the tutors' level of skills, is merely a prelude to adaptation by pastoral heads. Complaints of tutor 'unco-operativeness' often obscure absence of assessment of their needs, and of the way in which these can be met. This brings the discussion back to expectations as a key variable. Where expectations are rigid, Hersey and Blanchard point out that the style of management plays little part. Pastoral heads should look at the expectations tutors and pupils hold of them, and also at how they expect tutors and pupils to behave. Senior management's expectations have to be discussed as well as the pastoral heads' expectations of senior management. I suspect pastoral heads' expectations of the responses of senior management sometimes function as an unrecognised cause of limited behaviour. In training counsellors I use the concept of life space diagrams, stemming from the work of Lewin. Behaviour can be related directly to environmental dilemmas. Important components which should be assessed as part of diagnosis are the:

- goals towards which groups feel pulled;
- barriers or obstacles which impede the movement;
- paths along which they could move;
- restraining forces;
- coping possibilities.

Pastoral heads should map out these forces which influence development within *their own middle management team*; and within *each team of tutors led by a head of house or year*.

Examination of the differences *within* and *between* teams sparks off discussion and planning for what Lewin (1947) calls 'unfreezing'. Kelman's (1961) discussion of processes of social influence shows first a movement from compliance to identification motivated by the positive relations that have developed with the source of influence. This, in turn, becomes internalisation, because the new behaviours and values are felt to have been adopted voluntarily. Whatever the reality of Kelman's description, the pastoral head should be clear he or she is engaged in a process in which unfreezing is only a first step.

Howard *et al* follow up the theme of adaptation in leadership. In *Adaptive Counselling and Therapy* they also ask how much directive, and how much supportive, behaviour will be needed. Four styles of behaviour are identified:

1 Telling
2 Teaching
3 Supporting
4 Delegating

The assumption is that their effectiveness depends, in our case, on tutors' readiness for the task of development. Readiness is a product of the tutor's competence, confidence and willingness. In their discussion Howard *et al* recognise that under-direction in certain circumstances is as much a problem as is over-direction in others. Their framework indicates when one behaviour is likely to be more productive than the others.

1 *Telling* provides high direction and low support, and is claimed to be necessary when people are unwilling, unable and lack confidence. (One might well question this.)
2 *Teaching* provides both high direction and high support, and is useful when people are unable and unwilling.
3 *Supporting* gives low direction and high support, and is indicated when group members are able and willing but have little confidence.
4 *Delegating* is marked by low direction and low support, and can be productive when group members are able, willing and confident.

Readers should consult the works cited for themselves, asking 'What does this mean in my situation?'. No recipes are provided, but they create awareness of critical factors. Pastoral heads often feel damned if they do, and damned if they don't. Reddin and the others offer a way out of these paralysing confusions. We do not assume that nothing can or will change, but read the situation to see which approach gives the best choice of success.

Breaking into our learned helplessness
So much energy seems to go into stratagems for keeping disasters at arm's length rather than resolving them. Schmuck *et al* (1985) argued that organisational development helps the school develop 'a sustained capacity for solving its own problems'. How? The first step may well be analysis of the interaction and relationships *within* groups and *between* them. We are not concerned with the processes alone but the content: What is the interaction between pastoral heads and heads of academic departments about? Is it about learning, punishment or welfare? What is the significance of this for relationships? Jones, (1987) in a stimulating discussion of school leadership, rightly argues that it is inter-relatedness between groups which gives coherence to what happens in school.

Negotiation by pastoral heads leads to an agenda for development. Neat, predetermined plans have a seductive appeal, but what good are they when they ignore what teachers see as urgent, or when their perceived needs are passed over? Lewis (1985) stresses that the first step is collection of data. In pastoral development, after the starting point has been agreed, the agenda could be:

1 Investigation of the views held by pupils and parents about the nature of pastoral work, and searching for ways in which both groups could contribute to it. Pastoral guidance could be a tripartite exercise now that we are beginning to recognise the importance and benefits of parental involvement.

2 Analysis of the relative frequency of different types of offences that call for disciplinary reactions, and the adequacy of the measures taken to deal with them.

3 Action research into absenteeism based on the thesis that a school may be contributing to the problem but also has the power to ameliorate it. Jones (1980) reports how the measures taken improved attendance in her school from 77.5% in September 1974 to 88% in September 1977. Dawson (1982) and O'Hara *et al* (1982) describe Teacher Information Packages, and strategies for the assessment and intervention phases and target setting.

Problem solving springs from school-based study: a message we tend to ignore when pressure pushes us into a reactive position. But the school-based study actually relieves some of that pressure, and as Lewis points out, staff who feel less pressured are more likely to innovate. If communication becomes more open because it is not tied to a hierarchical structure, it leads to greater involvement in development. This reflects Schmuck *et al*'s view that needs for affiliation, influence and achievement have to be met if worthwhile development is to occur. Lewis helpfully illustrates the directness of a counselling approach to organisational development when she says the investigation should not be about:

- parent–teacher associations but *attitudes to teachers*
- pastoral structures but *attitudes to care*
- the organisation of teaching groups but *labelling*

We could begin by simple exploratory activities which encourage collaborative enquiry. Tutors use self-observation, keeping a diary of events related to the topic. Then the tutor group discusses with its leader the significance of the findings, allowing the next step or steps to emerge and be clarified. The leader's skills are used to sharpen the sense of direction, avoiding 'drift', or checking unbridled enthusiasm from leading members into premature action.

Another simple starting point is for partners to assess the strengths and weaknesses of pastoral work as it currently operates in the house or year. The leader gathers points as *pairs* report back, putting them on a flip chart and inviting comments from others. Then a decision is made about the next step.

Work in small groups is very productive. Role play is threatening to some teachers or dismissed by others as unrealistic, but they will discuss problems and plans honestly and openly in a supportive small group. Participants work in threes: one explains the problem or goal as precisely as possible. The other two then set out to assist her or him, looking at possibilities after the problem has been analysed, anticipating difficulties and inoculating against the tendency to claim that it is an impossible task. The behavioural counselling principles that we help people discover how they defeat themselves, and spell out the steps they can take are used here. The aim is also reinforcement of confidence that solutions exist and to generate hypotheses for consideration.

In two part courses at the Cambridge Institute of Education I have found it profitable to link them through observational and developmental training tasks in which participants tested out their ideas, seeking feedback from colleagues and pupils. They then shared experiences in part two and provided further mutual support. Small group work of this kind over a longer period, and amongst colleagues, leads to a sense of purpose and movement through this process of continuous testing of ideas, reporting back and evolvement of new steps. Each member in turn occupies the role of helped and helper. Attitudes and predictions unfreeze more easily when this mutual help exists and participants can relax from their public postures in staff and larger meetings.

Introductory activities could profitably examine the attitudes and behaviours which accentuate the divide between the pastoral and the curricular. *Part* of one such exercise is set out below to indicate a way of tackling this.

The structural elements which contribute to success or failure

1 Discuss the following in relation to your school:
  (i) The separation or integration of the pastoral and curricular.
    • How consciously does what is done in pastoral work relate to classroom activity and active learning?

- How does pastoral activity aid the teacher's job satisfaction?
- How are the links reinforced in your school?

(ii) What seem to be the dominant elements?
- The 'abortive punishment' approach, the 'inferior welfare' system and routine administration are examples of some negative tendencies.
- The belief that pastoral care is the task of the head of year or house rather than of the tutor.

2 What is the balance between preventive and after-the-event work?

Objectives of pastoral work

1 Discuss how clear your *long-run* objectives are. They give direction and purpose.
  (i) If asked, 'How would the school be different if pastoral care were taken away?', what would your answer be?
  (ii) What is it that pastoral activity contributes to the *output* of the school?

2 Now appraise your intermediate objectives which:
  (i) State what is done in each year, and what knowledge and skills have to be acquired.
  (ii) Relate each year's work to the preceding one, and prepare for the succeeding one, giving a sense of purpose and movement.
  (iii) Involve negotiation of the content of a tutor programme with the relevant academic departments eg social education, religious education, biology, drama, etc.

Job specifications

1 Discuss the job specifications of pastoral heads in your school. Ask:
  (i) What *assumptions* about the nature of pastoral care do they embody?

(ii) Are those assumptions sterile or out of date?
(iii) Do they fit the reality of everyday life in school?
      What are the implications if they do not?
2 What values are embodied in the job specification of
   the form tutor? Is the bias professional and creative,
   or mechanistic, perhaps sterile?

Expectations

1 Discuss this statement of a year head, 'I agree with
   the need for something different, but I can't change.
   My colleagues *expect* me to 'lam' into pupils when
   they are sent to me, and if I don't, they will think I've
   gone soft!'
2 Are the expectations of colleagues in your school
   helpful to (a) the year/house head, and (b) the tutor?
3 Are the expectations which impinge on you helpful,
   constricting, supportive or dismissive?
4 How would you modify unhelpful expectations which
   operate in your school?

Discuss the following statements about evaluation:

(i)   It is a team-based process.
(ii) It deepens gradually, as meanings emerge.
(iii) It demands careful thought and a planned
      approach in which techniques suited to the circum-
      stances are developed and used with increasing
      precision.
(iv) It takes new forms as the school's pastoral work
      develops.
(v)   It involves consideration of the school as a social
      system: what works in one school will not
      necessarily work in another.

TVEI and TRIST helpfully boosted teachers' awareness of their contribution to change and the power of so-called 'bottom-up' innovation. The necessary self-evaluation began by asking apparently simple questions, such as

1 Where are we now?
2 Where do we want to go?
3 How do we get there?

'Bottom-up' not only sounds murky but is inadequate without 'top-down' action which stimulates and supports changes coming from class teachers. There is no guarantee that the first two questions will produce change unless the answers to the third figure prominently and senior management clear the paths to development. Schmuck *et al* advocate STP analysis:

Situation   What are the current difficulties? (It seems at least as important to detect strengths and areas of success which can be springboards for development.)
Target state   What would you like to include that you are not doing? What do you want to do more of, or do better?
Path   What could you do or would you do to change things for the better? (Discussion will probably highlight possibilities, using means/ends thinking to detect the most economical path to the goals, and to evaluate the relative merits and costs of different proposals.)

A way of introducing this means/end approach is to get small groups to specify what they would regard as a worthwhile state of affairs in pastoral activity. They then work out the steps that will have to be taken to arrive at the desired state. Large sheets of paper are used for recording. Each group approaches another, seeking and giving supportive feedback.

This, and the other methods, break into learned helplessness and weaken reliance on perceptions of facing an impossible task: 'There isn't enough time', or 'Nothing will change!'. Confidence is built up because tutors realise that what they are doing in group work, is what will be demanded from pupils in tutor periods. The discussion is concrete and specific, concerned with situations that a teacher regards as important, such as confrontations in the classroom, attitudes to homework or problems of profiling.

Pastoral heads should face the fact that although small groups facilitate co-operative interaction and explore common problems, this does not mean uniformity and agreement will exist. Skilful leadership accepts that differences will exist, and allows a measure of autonomy to teachers. There is no reason why tutors should all be doing the same thing at the same time in the same way. Such variation does not do away with the need for accountability and justification, but strengthens them. It is autonomy and individuality within clearly defined limits which have come from consultation and negotiation. I have sometimes felt that pastoral heads overvalue affability and the impression of consensus as a sign of well-being. When one looks a little more deeply there are indications that the *apparent* good relationships are just that. A tacit agreement has developed that no one will rock the boat. The pleasant sense of agreement functions as a defence against self-evaluation or as a way of keeping the situation 'safe' and avoiding development. It is the equivalent of early closure on problems, the tendency to trivialise them by saying, 'The problem is just...', or 'All he needs is...', and immediate categorisation which blocks admission of contrary evidence. Those who rely on such mechanisms have found the toleration of doubt and uncertainty too anxiety-provoking to sustain. They then maintain a mask of good relationships, investing energy in this which could be used more profitably, whilst the problems that should be tackled are pushed out of sight. What to the outsider is patently ineffective, perhaps absurd, is justified by 'this is our way of doing things'. Pastoral heads *as a group* should look determinedly for the possibility of such distortions of reality, and then support one another as they open up the issues with tutors.

Classroom interaction

Pastoral activity should feed into the classroom. Tutors should take what they do in the tutor period into their subject teaching, applying and extending it. But is it so easy? Despite welcome and heartening innovations in the last few years, divisiveness and territory are still prominent features of school life. Can we integrate pastoral and curricular activity if pupils see them as unconnected, perhaps contradictory? Fifth year pupils have reported difficulty in accepting pastoral claims of caring when they feel ways of resolving pupil-teacher differences are unjust, or that pastoral activities do not meet their needs for responsibility or recognise their maturity. Daily experience encourages pupils to see life in school as a collection of unrelated events: they attend a lesson; the bell rings; they then study another subject until the bell rings again. The impression is given that each subject is a discrete entity having little relation with others. The rigid attitudes of certain teachers, including those of pastoral heads tied to out-of-date models of pastoral care, have made the pastoral and curricular separate territories between which a gulf is fixed that people have given up trying to bridge or that they take for granted.

Pastoral heads will find it helpful to work with colleagues, sharpening their perceptions of what occurs in their classroom, and using counselling skills to improve quality of classroom life. Counselling skills create the open-mindedness which facilitates active learning and problem solving. Modern curriculum developers do not limit themselves to the development of a well-stocked mind with the capacity for using knowledge, but wish to extend students' range of operations, such as detecting problems as much as resolving them, or using texts and learning experiences to generate new ideas. Unfortunately, students often feel unready or unwilling to accept this conception of learning. Counselling recognises the impact that feeling has on thinking; accepting that feelings of inadequacy, over-sensitivity to praise or blame or the fear of creating adverse impressions in authority figures may inhibit the capacity to construct and test hypotheses. Counselling insists we take the context into account, rather than narrowly focus on the learning behaviours.

Development builds the teacher's capacity to analyse at different levels. It is valid to talk of the class climate in an overall way, yet we need to map what is happening at the individual, sub-group and total group perspectives. Brophy and Good (1974) remind us there are as many classroom climates as individuals. Each student interacts differently with the teacher, each meets different responses from peers, and has her or his sources of reward and threat. We should be alert to this. A class is not just an aggregate of individuals, it contains sub-groups bonded together through friendship or shared characteristics, eg Sumner and Warburton's (1972) industrious or 'allergic' to school groups. Unthinkingly, due to the pressure of classroom life, we can respond to sub-groups in a way which stresses, even invites, the development of a shared identity based in opposition. A halo effect influences our judgements and reactions, maintaining students' negative attitudes and behaviours. Heads of year or house have often made a profitable start on linking the pastoral and the curricular by examining classroom interaction. What is it in a particular class or age group which encourages pupils to abdicate individual responsibility, and succumb to the pressures of a sub-group which rewards rejection of teacher influence? How do we contribute to this? Topping (1983) cites evidence which suggests that teacher interaction with students is more weighted towards the negative than they know. Kolvin *et al* (1981) reported that praise and positive attention are given more sparsely than the teacher realised: encouragingly, they also found that discussion and training rectified this. Tutors find it helpful to assess whether the negative comments are directed at individuals or more vaguely at the class. Do the sub-groups attract them? This is not trivial: if older students find *public* praise noxious (see, for example, Hargreaves, 1967 and Topping, 1983) it is still possible to build up a positive image of the class through praise. Pastoral activity is concerned to build positive group identity as much as individual ones.

The conscientious teacher worries about being 'unable to reach' certain students or feeling she or he cannot deal competently or constructively with their behaviours in class. Pastoral heads and their tutors should see wrestling with these problems as part of pastoral care for teachers. We must press for time to explore the reasons for, and the reality of, such stressful feelings, starting with our criteria for success and failure in the classroom and the accuracy of our perceptions of it. What shapes our assessments of ourselves: some imaginary audience whose later judgements have to be taken into account? Over-perfectionist standards? Or a simplistic notion of teaching? Developers accept that inner feeling may be incongruent with outer reality, for example, individuals honestly confess to uncertainty and anxiety when the external observer would assess them as competent and secure in their role. Developers therefore are sensitive to possible discrepancies between self-assessment and appraisal by others – something to be considered as staff appraisal develops. Discussion of these perspectives as an example of disjunction between 'my view of your view of me' (Laing *et al* 1966) seems crucial for meaningful appraisal. Let us take the point a little further. We interpret our own behaviour through our knowledge of our inner life and our relevant past history. Those observing us give it meaning by referring to general beliefs about how people ought to behave in the particular situation, or assuming that our reactions will be similar to theirs, or by comparing us with others.

The message is that how we see things largely determines the way we behave. Frieze *et al*(1983) take the stand that perceptions of performance are important determinants of teachers' classroom behaviours. Certainly, if profiling is to assume creative forms, then teachers' awareness in the area of perception will have to be deepened. Meanwhile it will be sensible to build awareness through discussion of the following:

1 What do they see as success or failure – in the classroom specifically, and in teaching generally?
2 What are the purposes of comparisons made by the teacher of himself or herself with colleagues? What are the costs? Comparisons seem to be inevitable, although we balk at admitting this. Their functions and costs are manifold; eg provision of self-satisfaction, the strengthening of professional helplessness or providing a measuring stick.
3 What do they believe is controllable and modifiable in students' behaviour and what cannot be changed? The element of 'can' in the causes of behaviour is crucial: effort is seen as within the student's control, whilst ability is not. Attribution of lack of ability relieves the teacher of responsibility to some degree, while lack of effort poses problems of motivation and control. Intent influences the teacher's reactions: students are more likely to be sharply reprimanded when the teacher believes they intended to commit the offence, ie the behaviour was under the student's control.
4 How does the teacher boost his or her self-worth? This is salient in an era of devaluation, pressure and coping with difficult incidents whilst feeling unsupported. Is there a danger of restricting our roles and limiting our aspirations *when*, as the work initiated by the Cambridge Institute of Education and other sources demonstrates, teachers can initiate very positive developments (see Holly and Whitehead, 1984 and 1986; Somekh *et al*, 1987 and Reid *et al*, 1987)?
5 Closely associated with self-worth is assessment of the threats to, and erosion of, the teacher's job satisfaction and sense of professionalism. Our needs for success are blocked by the forces outlined above. Debilitating stress occurs when we feel we cannot be the kind of teacher we want to be. The combined frustration and exhaustion pushes some into cynicism; more become inflexible, perhaps automatically resorting to routine punishments which merely maintain the sterile relationships with pupils presenting difficulties. Reciprocity in relationships means that if one partner changes, the other may well modify. If, in a supportive context, we have the courage to ask (and teachers *are* courageous) 'What is our contribution to these things we deplore?' we free ourselves from the feeling of being victims of events.

6 Another facet of classroom interactions is illuminated by Heider's (1958) thesis that attributions of intent and motive are highly subjective. But do we tackle this aspect of judgement? Our judgements of ourselves, colleagues and students are deeply influenced by our perceptions of:

- what ought to be;
- what one would like to be;
- what is.

Failure to examine the discrepancies between them, and then work out their significance, leaves us prey to anxiety, guilt or defensive scapegoating of others. As a group we should examine the discrepancies, working out ways of dealing with their consequences, and ensuring that we take a critical view of our judgements rather than assuming they are objective.

Pastoral and academic heads should work together in helping colleagues deal with the six points. Discussion of them may seem a luxury, even irrelevant, in stressful times, yet I am convinced that this human relations approach is essential for development in pastoral care.

Involvement of pupils

GCSE allows students to make decisions about learning, requiring group work and group problem solving. Pastoral care, if it is not to be an educational dinosaur, should contribute to these changes in classroom roles. Consumer research should be increasingly applied to the development of the pastoral programme; not solely as one source of information about relevant content (Hamblin, 1978 and 1983), but as a way of extending the sense of ownership of it to students. Sometimes I doubt if tutors have any sense of ownership of the pastoral programme despite the emphasis placed on the concept by TVEI and TRIST. Active involvement of students in determining the content and producing materials may be an antidote to the disenchantment of fourth and fifth year students reported by Hamblin (1984).

Here are illustrations of what I have met:

- Sixth and fifth year students have helped with the induction programme and learning in the first year, eg Williams (1981) and Melling (1987).
- Third year pupils have undertaken presentations based on

investigations into work in the neighbourhood, involving parents and family friends. The fieldwork was done in their free time; the tape recordings of interviews, posters and photographs were excellent. Enthusiasm and confidence were high.

- First year sixth form students have helped fifth years to cope with anxieties and frustrations associated with the anxieties of public examinations, and the tensions raised by the contrary pressures of school, home and peer group.

These informal agents of guidance had a credibility that came from their closeness to the experience. We do not have to do it all: students taking art and drama apply their skills, producing first-rate cartoons, posters, diagrams, audio or video recordings with zest; the fact that they are to be used in their year group acting as a spur to excellence. In two-part CFPS courses, teachers have prepared modules of activities as an interim task. They tested them out in their schools, inviting students' evaluations and suggestions for improvement and further activities. For a few, this involvement of the students created apprehension; but many more were exhilarated by the experience. Students lost their feeling that tutor work was superficial activity imposed on them: they felt they were partners in a meaningful process; responsible co-operation was a reality.

But could not these methods link pastoral work to the class-room? GCSE and CPVE require self-evaluation, target-setting and initiative. Tutor periods could provide preliminary practice in these things. Marland *et al* (1981) make the crucial point that learning in context needs to be accompanied by the didactic – creating awareness through discussion of the processes employed by the learner. Feelings about co-operation, competition and communication should be explored. Kolb (1984) argues that ideas are formed and reformed through experience; that learning is a process of *creating* knowledge. He sees four cyclical stages of concrete experience, reflective observation, abstract conceptualisation and active experimentation. Tutor periods should be concerned with reflective observation and conceptualisation, in which students build personal theories of learning. Many of them currently rely on second hand simple formulae about learning which are devoid of personal meaning. Pastoral heads can learn much from the stimulating work of Lorac and Weiss (1981). Pastoral and academic heads work together on this, freeing tutor periods from the grip of endless worksheets which invite boredom and superficiality.

A two-way process has to be encouraged: pastoral heads see the activities of the pastoral periods as hopefully influencing classroom attitudes and behaviour; insufficient attention is given to classroom research which could shape the pastoral programme. This two-way engagement in a developmental exercise encourages student responsibility for learning and allows the teacher to escape from the perception of the class as an inert mass which has to be acted on. Joint activity will be essential to allow the National Curriculum to be sensitive to the needs of individuals. Fifth year pupils may also get the responsibility and recognition they regard as essential to take seriously the claims of 'caring'.

Without this adaptive approach, peer group interaction which has a coercive force strengthens as pupils move through the school. Dependency on the diktats of the peer group increases. Surrender of responsibility and abdication of individual identity for reliance on a group-derived identity – stressing opposition to adults generally and authority figures specifically – is a not uncommon temporary phenomenon in adolescence. Peer groups meet vital needs for affiliation and recognition. Unfortunately, this creates negative tensions between the demands of school and pupils' social lives. These tensions are often expressed in some variation of: 'If you did everything the teachers want you to do, you'd have no life of your own.' How can this be handled? Paradoxically, the solution is to give pupils greater responsibility in pastoral and academic work. Why, when pupils are given, accept and fulfil responsibilities in the primary school, do we not consistently build on this in the secondary school? Identity by opposition is essentially infantile because one's responses are shaped by what is being imposed: when it changes the opposer has to change. Note that it may have temporary value in adolescent development; the continued reliance on identity by opposition stimulated by our actions is the object of debate. Why does the allegedly caring activity of pastoral care deny the reality of the massive development in early and middle adolescence by *not* adjusting its methods, increasing responsibility, and stimulating enterprise and challenge?

Taking the standpoint of pupils encourages us to ask how they evaluate us. Hamblin (1984) found that first year pupils stress that teachers should be able to control unruly pupils, know and keep the school rules, be punctual and punish fairly. Signs of preparation command respect from pupils as evidence of the teacher's commitment. The self as a learner – a major part of the output of the school – intricately relates to classroom environments which make statements about the nature of those who work in them. Audience anxiety (Buss, 1980) dogs the adolescent. Fear of being 'shown-up' is strong. Phillips' (1978) analysis of anxiety and achievement reminds us to take into account fear of assertiveness and self-expression, anxiety about tests, lack of confidence in meeting the expectations of others and physiological reactions associated with low tolerance of stress. Staff development extends our knowledge, facilitating better teaching and classroom relationships. Deepened understanding of underlying causes of behaviour (for example, a pupil's reaction to stress can take many forms: avoidance of other demanding situations, denial that stress exists, reactive or displaced aggression or near obsessional concentration on work) allows us to apply our professional skills more precisely. Questions addressed to pupils may activate feelings of inadequacy, reinforce hypocrisy by unintentionally encouraging socially desirable or untrue answers, or convince them that they must produce *the* right answer. Sex bias enters; Stanworth (1983) argues that manifold forces operate in the classroom to activate and sustain gender differences. Apparently more favourable treatment of girls may have long-run debilitating effects whilst the sensitive and caring side of the boys may be denied legitimacy. Limited and rigid forms of questioning invite unthinking regurgitation of facts, giving the appearance of learning, without the substance. Good pastoral work is rooted in exploration of these matters.

Other aspects of classroom interaction related to pastoral development
Classroom interaction has an honourable educational history, yet the legacy of past work which over-concentrated on verbal behaviours – a limited element in classroom interaction – is still with us, obscuring as much as it illuminates. Anderson *et al's* (1945; 1946) concepts of dominative and integrative styles of teaching are still vital: their weakness is that they tend to assume pupils are merely responsive. In reality, many problems arise from pupils' negative definitions of learning situations, their ploys for dealing with them, and the almost automatic attribution by some of hostile intent to the teacher. Bellack *et al* (1966) used a game-like analysis of moves and countermoves: soliciting, responding, structuring and reacting. This makes a good basis for the analysis of difficult classroom situations, *provided* that the impact of predictions and attribution of intent are included. Predictions, of course, are inevitable but lead to unthinking categorisations of pupils and behaviour.

Berne (1964) highlighted the prevalence of games in human relationships which are fundamentally self-defeating. Pastoral heads get trapped in games of 'I'm only trying to help!', 'I'm different from all the others', or 'Come to me, and I'll solve your problems'. They should look at what activates defensive moves in pupils in the upper school who feel legitimate professional boundaries are being breached – 'Nosy-parker teachers asking questions no teacher has a right to ask'. Some exhaust themselves in the abortive alleged 'caring' of a few individuals, never questioning the validity *and* utility of this. What they probably achieve is the creation of a network of interaction which perpetuates the problem. Are they dependent on such pupils for confirmation that their role is justifiable?

Analysis of the nature and purpose of moves initiated by pupils, and the outcome of responses by teachers, leads to useful insights in staff development. How do pupils interpret and respond to the teacher's action? Does the teacher use all the ways of responding open to her or him? Pressures to maintain order in the classroom may freeze perceptions, leading to early closure on situations which unhelpfully restricts actions, or allows difficult pupils to reduce the teacher to impotence. Appreciation of the ways in which both sides block, divert or nullify the moves of others leads to better decision making and classroom interaction.

Classroom decisions are, for the greater part, routine and intuitive unless the grossly unexpected occurs (Calderhead, 1984). If, as the FEU argues, guidance and counselling is to be integrated into the curriculum, then we have to be aware realistically that pupils may not respond positively. The thrust of GCSE is laudable, but some pupils are unequipped and unwilling to meet the new demands for planning, organisation and responsibility: passivity holds attractive rewards for some learners. Is it not odd that teachers' resistance to change is recognised, but we naïvely assume that pupils will welcome our innovations? Yet they have effective mechanisms for disregarding them or distancing themselves, for example, the casual nonchalance described by Woods (1985) which the infuriated teacher finds almost impossible to change. Bennett and Desforges (1985) cite Doyle (1979; 1983) who stresses the reciprocal adaptations between teachers and their pupils: the latter quickly learn what teachers want, producing at least the semblance of it; their teachers adapt imperceptibly to what pupils offer. Gender influences are at work. Males tend to accept more readily the excuses of girls or succumb to their emotional blackmail. Woods (1985) and Measor and Woods (1984) offer lively descriptions of the mechanisms used by girls to manipulate both teachers and peers. Both sexes shrewdly assess and use tactics which shape teachers' behaviour. They force adherence to the implicit norms of interaction by 'turning nasty', avoiding eye contact or appearing indifferent. Doyle (1979) directs attention to pupils' power to change exploratory and experiential learning activities into more dependent experience. Objections and a barrage of questions or signals of anxiety compel the teacher to give encompassing guidelines, defining what she or he wants, relieving the pupil of responsibility for his or her learning. These matters should be at the forefront of our discussions making learning an active dialogue between teacher and teacher, pupils and teachers and pupil and pupil.

Egglestone (1979) suggests we have incomplete knowledge of the influences which shape teachers' decisions in the classroom. Inclusion of this topic in staff development for pastoral care certainly facilitates integration of the pastoral and curricular: in training courses teacher decision making has been a productive starting point.

First we assess our *preferences* as decision-makers; *style* may be too strong, and gives insufficient weight to situational factors. *Preferences* based in personality and past experience interact with *situations* to shape our decisions.

1 Using recent concrete incidents – reaction to parental actions, a grave misdemeanour by a pupil, the decision to refer to the schools' psychological services or social services – we examine in small groups our tendencies towards pre-categorisation, interpretation of motives, preferences for information from certain sources and other forms of selectivity.
2 Is there a danger that threat exists in certain situations which we prefer to avoid by not dealing with them – or that we act without regard for the complexities?
3 We should learn to question our assumptions about the motives and intent of others. They may be erroneous but we still act on them, creating a self-fulfilling prophecy.

It is not self-indulgent to question our decisions: it is vital for effectiveness. Beliefs about what works, and what will not work have to be scrutinised rationally. Pressures of time push us towards short-run or expedient decisions which bring later problems. The teacher is driven by the twin pressures of conforming to a professional image and the constraints imposed by accommodation to organisational practices. Survival techniques such as distancing oneself from the needs of pupils, or the desperate ploy of 'get them before they get you' become commonplace. Expectations of colleagues have a compulsive quality despite their diminishing of individual spontaneity and enterprise. The deadening impact of expectations is strong in some schools: their hold will continue until staff development legitimises discussion of the validity and nature of expectations. In pastoral work conflict usually centres on which expectations are proper and which obligations have priority.

What is it in the organisation which forces immature responses from responsible, intelligent professionals? False definitions of a crisis may reduce the head of year or house to giving trivial reprimands to pupils, and because they have to leave classes to deal with super-ficialities, their credibility as teachers is questioned by pupils. Shortage of time is stressed; but how much work is done on management of time? Either/or thinking maintains false dichotomies, for example, which is to be honoured first: responsibility as a subject teacher or as a tutor? To whom is concern to be given: the pupil presenting behavioural difficulties or the form as a group? The problems are real and opinions have to be vented, and through this the false polarity of separation of the pastoral and curricular has to be tackled.

Classroom decisions frequently relate to problems of control. Hargreaves (1979) provides an insightful account on decisions and associated control techniques. He draws attention to the un-questioned assumptions about the needs of disadvantaged pupils which stress behavioural regulation at the cost of intellectual independence and academic achievement. The decisions made before a lesson begins are significant for interaction in the lesson. Too often, they are made rigidly, being determined by intuitive beliefs, which are then justified by stereotypical statements about pupils' expectations and needs. Calderhead (1984) discusses *preactive* decisions which focus on the subject matter to be covered, the sequence in which items are introduced, the apparatus and materials to be used, the participa-tion required from pupils, and the general expectations of pupils' responses and achievement. Our discussion relates to tutor work primarily, but we should apply it to our subject teaching. Discussion includes:

1 Teachers' decisions about teaching methods and types of activity are shaped by the need to anticipate colleagues' reactions to the noise involved. Violation of accepted norms about noise level is one

example of constraints on teachers' decisions. What other factors inhibit teachers' decisions? Is there an implicit consensus within the school about the way lessons should be conducted, especially about the social distance between teachers and pupils?

Differences of approach which are too marked arouse anxiety, even suspicion and rejection in colleagues. Do these considerations influence our decisions about taking up new ideas? Is a neglected, yet key area, the need for negotiation about the range of variation in methods?

2 What is the balance between tutors' input and pupils' activity? How is this determined? Can we justify the balance, or are we unthinkingly relying on the assumption that pupil activity must necessarily be 'a good thing'? Do we undervalue thought and reflection in tutor work?

3 Do we over-rely on a meticulously prepared pastoral programme which denies tutors the opportunity to innovate, and gain a sense of ownership. Does it allow pupils to take some responsibility for their own guidance, and see the pastoral programme *as a joint endeavour between tutor and form*?

4 Are we guilty of treating the tutor group as homogeneous, offering little opportunity for choice of activity by individuals or small groups?

5 Have we made considered decisions about the adaptation of methods and content to meet the rapid growth of maturity in the adolescent?

What if the school contains a large number of allegedly less-able pupils who come from disadvantaged backgrounds? Hargreaves (1979) shows that in such conditions the intellectual side of classroom work is submerged by what could loosely be called the moral. I believe that tutor work is just as vulnerable to this tendency. The content of tutor work could be saturated by justifications for what happens in the pastoral system and school. Again and again I have seen tutors forgetting the purpose of activities, and retreating to injunctions which have little, if any, impact on pupils: 'If we all did this, then ...' or 'When you do get out into the world ...'. (Note the curious assumption that school is not of the world!) The strong tinge of prudential morality is not to be dismissed lightly. The relevant question, however, is about the effectiveness of the behaviour described, and how we develop co-operation, altruism and the capacity for standpoint-taking as forms of moral behaviour.

Osgood, Suci and Tannenbaum argue that perceptions and judgements have three basic dimensions:

Evaluation (good versus bad)
Potency (strong versus week)
Activity (active versus passive)

It has often been humbling to assess my own decisions in the light of these bi-polar dimensions. In training exercises, participants helpfully become aware of over-sensitivity to the implications of weakness or passivity in their decisions. Closer inspection of the evaluatory element often follows: it is liberating when they discover the degree to which their decision making is dominated by unrealistic comparisons with others, or impossible images of perfection. Participants usually become aware of the 'hidden audience' whose later evaluations have to be kept in mind. The impact of the frustration caused by an unwanted compromise and the sense of not being faithful to their principles are examined. The advantages of honest discussion of this becomes apparent: the implicit and immature dependency is seen for what it is, a hangover from earlier adolescent needs for affiliation and approval.

Key questions about decisions are:

1 To what do we respond in the classroom or tutor group? Why?
2 To what do we respond in face-to-face situations? Why do these behaviours or attitudes of the individual assume salience?
3 Are there marked differences in our responses in groups and with an individual?
4 What makes us feel it is imperative to act?
5 When, and why, do we feel it is better to ignore behaviours?
6 Evidence is provided by Sutcliffe and Whitfield (1979) that inexperienced teachers make more immediate decisions, whilst experienced teachers deal with similar situations through reflective decisions, avoiding immediate action and getting into a position where withdrawal would mean loss of face. There is no necessary or inevitable connection between the reduction of impulsive decisions and improved classroom control: too many other factors are operating! One possibility is that there *may* be male and female differences in processing information and ways of reaching a conclusion. Males as a group may be more vulnerable to threatened loss of status whilst women have different anxieties. Let us be clear, however, that there are more differences within each sex, than

between them. The differences that do exist may well be due more to social forces than innate differences. Taylor (1979) studying primary school teachers, found that authoritarian males tend to minimise the distinctions between the traits they use in judging pupils. Women may well tend to be more complex and sophisticated in their assessments of behaviour and personality. Be that as it may, there is enough evidence to suggest that pastoral work, especially in the areas of profiling and assessment, would gain from probing discussion of real versus assumed similarities or differences. What is it that strengthens the tendency to make simplistic assessments of risks and probabilities in decision making? To ask what makes for open and cognitively complex assessments of problems, rather than over-simplify them, is even more vital.

Teacher decision making begins, at least implicitly, with a definition of a goal to be achieved, or recognition of a problem that should be dealt with. Year or house heads should take problems that concern tutors, helping them reach and then implement decisions. Tutors should engage with these questions:

1 Is our definition or perception of the nature of the problem (eg absenteeism or disruptive behaviour) accurate? Have we focused on certain things eg home conditions, to the exclusion of others? How does it appear in classroom, peer group or elsewhere?

   If we wish to attempt change of attitude or behaviour of a small sub-group in the classroom, have we anticipated all the difficulties and assessed all the possibilities? Assessment of the context of the problem is essential, eg what are the likely reactions of other pupils if the desired changes occur?

2 Are we acting on predictions unsupported by evidence? Hamblin (1974, 1984, 1986) emphasises the importance of helping pupils assess the nature and consequences of their predictions in learning and group interaction. The teacher's predictions are also crucial: if we predict that a problem will escalate, or that other pupils will imitate, then we feel immediate firm action is necessary.

3 Reliance on simple recipes for dealing with problems is not necessarily ineffective. Group discussions open up the opportunity for evaluation of our reactions and discovery that we have taken for granted what is questionable.

4 We have seen that decisions may be shaped by a 'hidden audience' whose later judgements have to be kept in mind. We belong to

sub-groups in the school in which attitudes and opinions are shared as part of the group identity. Changes seen as theatening (eg insecurity from amalgamation, perhaps accompanied by loss of status) increase emotional dependence on the sub-group, whose members use irrational pressures against those who seem to be wavering in their allegiance, trying to ensure they conform to the 'group think'.

5 Staff development requires evaluation of post-decisional reactions. There is a tendency to justify a course of action once we implement it, leading to exaggerated devaluation of the rejected possibilities. Festinger (1957) and Brehm and Cohen (1962) suggest we search for, and select, information which supports what we have done. The bias which results is ignored, indeed we may not fully apprehend the existence of this bolstering process. Where initial emotions ran high, the bolstering effect is at its strongest. Case studies involving confidentiality, ethical questions about intervention or pupils' sexual difficulties bring awareness of these processes to the forefront.

The school as a social system

The relegation of pastoral activity to abortive punishment, emotional first-aid or minor administration is psychological myopia stemming from lack of awareness of the school as a social system. Parsons and Shils (1951) highlight the crucial characteristics of a social system:

1 A *process of interaction* between two or more people is involved.
2 These people are *oriented towards the goals* to be pursued, and the *means for pursuing those goals*:

- *Roles* and *constellations of roles* are developed.
- *Expectations* about the behaviour of role holders emerge.

Let us examine these elements. Patterns of interaction develop which serve hidden purposes, for example, pastoral heads criticise tutors for being unco-operative. Investigation may reveal that those pastoral heads actually maintain the unco-operativeness by failing to consult or involve tutors in decisions about members of the form, or *reducing* the significance of the role in the eyes of pupils. The observer might find it difficult to reject the conclusion that a change in the deplored behaviours would actually be unwelcome because the pastoral head would have to take on new responsibilities and extend his or her skills. Tutor and head of year or house may, in practice, be in unwitting collusion to keep pastoral work at a low level.

Interaction becomes sterile when the vaunted communication is distorted by unchallenged sub-group affiliations which falsely attribute negative motives to others. Chapter One illustrated the ways in which relations between role holders can be complex, contradictory or antagonistic: avoidance of systematic analysis of them perpetuates the sterility, and change becomes a remote prospect.

Social systems are given structure by sub-systems which have physical and psychological territory and boundaries. Richardson (1973) emphasises the importance of transactions across the boundaries of sub-systems. Staff development requires examination of what occurs in the various sub-systems – academic, pastoral, managerial and ancillary. Action *within* and *between* the sub-systems illuminates the forces which inhibit change: boundary transactions between the academic and pastoral may incorporate definitions of 'a crisis' which allow the subject teacher to abdicate responsibility, and ensure that pastoral heads are tied to giving trivial reprimands. Transactions across the boundary of the school with parents and neighbourhood have always been potentially sensitive but recent years have seen them become the foci for anxiety; staff development will include improved understanding of them. Consistent monitoring and improvement of them is a priority. Remarkably, many teachers appear unaware of the way myths about a school develop in a catchment area; although they themselves have rigid beliefs about the reactions of parents, they do little to correct misinterpretations of policies, and false perceptions of the teacher's work.

Key processes
Bennett (1974) argues that the transmission of value-permeated behaviours is as central to teaching as giving knowledge. He questions whether the values of the school should over-ride those of parents. Pastoral heads and tutors should apply themselves to this theme. Complex issues are present: early closure on the problems is unprofessional. At the simplest level, is there a danger of teacher omnipotence? If parental values are limited or anti-developmental, has the school the right to extend them? Where does the independence of the adolescent enter? A book could be written on the topic but it should be constantly debated and reviewed by pastoral heads, not

solely because parental involvement could lead to a backward looking view of education, but because of the overlap between parental and pastoral roles. Equally, some parents may wish to surge ahead faster than some teachers deem wise. It is folly to talk as if parents are an undifferentiated group; discussion is only meaningful in relation to a particular group of parents and a specific school. The pastoral programme may well need to be a joint enterprise; parents not only having access to it but actively contributing; pupils should also be active participants in developing it. First, we need to research pupils' perceptions of the motive and intent of pastoral activity. Do they see it as an intrusive and impertinent form of paternalism or maternalism denying the rapid development of the adolescent years, and stifling their self-responsibility? Failure to come to terms with those things ensures that pastoral activity remains a facade fronting little of real moment.

Hargreaves (1982) argues that in our desire to boost individuality and reinforce autonomy we have fallen into the 'fallacy of individualism'. This is the educational equivalent of looking after the pence in the belief that the pounds will look after themselves. Maybe, in unthinking endorsement of individuality as desirable, we are as naïve as the young people who believe that sweeping away existing edifices will inevitably result in a just society. But is there necessarily conflict between learning and experiences which serve the general well-being in the larger society and that which promotes individual development? Conscience can be seen as inhibitory or as positively seeking to meet standards of excellence in relations with others. Writers on moral development incline to the view that self-respect is essential for truly responsible behaviour (see, for example, Kay 1968; Lickona (ed), 1976; Wright, 1971 and Williams and Williams, 1970). There is no necessary relationship between guilt and resistance to temptation. Whilst Aronfreed's (1968) view that children have to learn to behave in a socially-adaptive way – acquiring inner controls through anxiety and inhibiting responses – is a necessary one, it is not sufficient to account for altruism. Pastoral work is rooted in the development of positive self-image where pupils define themselves as the kind of person who is ready to help and unwilling to exploit. Pastoral work accepts the orientation to seek approval and avoid punishment as inevitable – all of us possess this – but tries to help pupils reach the 'principled' stage of morality described by Kohlberg (1976) in which people 'are ends in themselves and must be treated as such'.

The discussion merely illustrates, but should be sufficient to set pastoral heads thinking about their role in developing personal and social responsibility. Current approaches to the pastoral programme may ignore what Bradford and Cohen (1984) call 'over-arching goals'. These unifying goals bring a year or house together in a shared endeavour. Students see tutors co-operating, and each group has a part to play in achieving the goal. Identity by belonging to year or house then takes precedence over the form identity, but the crucial elements are involvement in achieving the group goal and experience of adolescents and adults co-operating together to achieve it. Producing a handbook which is sold for a worthy cause; a survey of neighbourhood needs; working to do something which helps the whole school are examples. In the later years, students should be given a major role in the planning, making our positive expectations of them clear. Parental involvement will increase the sense of shared endeavour: the spin-off may be that this modifies the tinge of defensiveness which still permeates parental meetings.

Rutter *et al* (1979) noted that similar actions had dissimilar outcomes in different schools. A climate of expectations develops through which behaviours are interpreted differently. Oppenheim (1966) modified the Lewinian statement that behaviour is a function of the environment to include perceptions of the environment. What we do is dependent on how we see things, but the value climate of the school partially determines what pupils and teachers see. They view events from different vantage points, but both are influenced by the pervasive value climate. Teachers are professionals: one requirement of the professional is that she or he takes the standpoint of his or her clients. It then becomes possible to assess how the value climate creates *probabilities* that certain actions and attitudes will operate, and how others are inhibited. The actions and attitudes that are encouraged contribute to the value climate that sustains them: a cyclical self-perpetuating force is at work almost unnoticed by teachers. Older pupils have sometimes understood them, but find it expedient to hide this. In passing, note that students should be helped to take the standpoints of teachers and other adults through the pastoral programme.

These forces, which appear intangible, at best elusive, are fundamental to pastoral development. They illustrate the Gestalt principle that the whole is more than the sum of the parts. At the simplest level, we can become aware of the power of gradually-emerging images which are independent of specific incidents: one product of the secondary school is the image of the teacher held by different groups of pupils. In one affluent area I recently found the image was that of the teacher as a 'loser' who was not getting the 'real money'. Therefore teachers were not to be taken seriously as credible sources of guidance. Teachers somewhat reluctantly admit they have largely implicit models of an ideal pupil. They see that the very amorphousness of such models shields them from rational analysis increasing their influence upon the teacher's judgements. Different implicit models exist for the sexes: a relevant factor in our struggle to reduce the impact of gender stereotypes in the classroom. GCSE demands pupil initiatives and independence, yet the implicit ideal pupil models often stress passive receptive learning: as with criterion-referenced assessment, teachers may find it harder than they realise to discard long-held frameworks of judgement. Heads of year and tutors benefit from action research which explores:

1 The reputations allocated to certain groups of pupils. What is the basis for this? Living in a particular neighbourhood; teachers' experience of their elder brothers or sisters; general beliefs operating in the school about what certain groups of pupils can and should learn?

2 Exploration of how pupils and certain teachers acquire deviant identities. Courage will be needed to explore this process operating on teachers, yet it is salutary to ask what causes a teacher to be categorised as inadequate, incompetent, unrealistic, a 'boat rocker' or unco-operative. What functions do such labels serve for those who allocate them, and what is the impact on the labelled? A prerequisite may be identification of current beliefs about normality – a singularly loose concept which we constantly use. King (1973) reminds us that 'good' is used both technically and morally, eg the term is applied to pupils' schoolwork and their behaviour. Examination of pupils whom we regard as exemplary, and teachers seen as effective by staff and pupils, will be productive provided we take the Mannheimian view outlined in Chapter One.

3 Checking our judgements through observation is useful action research. We have preconceived notions about the interaction between groups of pupils or individuals but, like staffroom beliefs about parents, they may have tenuous links with reality.

The goals of the school
King makes a helpful distinction between the instrumental and the expressive aspects of the school. The former is made up of the processes through which knowledge and skills are transmitted. This part of the school's output is increasingly closely scrutinised in relation to the needs of industry and the move towards a post-industrial society. Ansoff (1984) writes of the problems of industrial management in a turbulent and unpredictable age. Resistance to change exacerbates the discrepancy between the imperatives of the environment and the firm's capacity to cope. Schools are not immune to these forces yet may rely on past experience which is not a sound guide to the future. Careers education was widely neglected in the 1970s; now we have welcome links between industry and schools, work experience and greater appreciation of entrepreneurial skills. So far, so good: but if monitoring the instrumental side of the school implies that teachers should have an accurate concept of what is needed for a modern labour force, dangers exist. We could rely on the past where it is inappropriate because of the rate of change, and undervalue the expressive which is concerned with the inculcation of values and the wider creative aspects of adult life. King's conclusion that arguments about the purpose of education lie in disagreement about the relative value to be placed on the instrumental and expressive, needs taking up by pastoral heads. The two aspects of school life do not necessarily conflict; pastoral work contributes to both; alertness to the contradictions between them we unwittingly bring about, is required from pastoral heads as part of their contribution to curriculum development.

Handy and Aitken (1986) correctly stress the importance of the collective purpose of the school, but what is it in the current situation of imposed changes? We saw in Chapter One the existence of conflicting realities in pastoral work. How can the conflicting viewpoints and resistances be reconciled so that a common sense of purpose is established? Teachers care deeply, but job satisfaction eludes them; stress comes from the feeling that they cannot do the job as well as they wish – surely evidence of commitment? Management of teacher stress has to be tackled resolutely through co-operation by pastoral and academic heads. Without this, a semblance of unified pursuit of common goals will not manage to hide debilitating tensions. System based analysis usefully includes mapping the stresses falling on different groups of teachers; distinguishing between personally generated stress due to costly classroom decision making or lack of such skills as defusing difficult situations and those emanating from the school's educational organisation. (A later analysis and exercise takes up these points, see p. 145.)

Bennett (1974) distinguishes between short- and long-term goals. Short-term goals seem to be about survival, preventing oneself from being swamped when one feels bedevilled by a spate of new demands. Social and political forces conspire to increase unpredictability. The head in particular has to cope with a present permeated by problems and still plan for an uncertain future: Buckley (1988) stresses the need for creative vision in resolving the present/future dilemma. The lively discussion by Jones (1987) suggests that heads feel stressed because of the demands for conflict resolution and negotiation skills they have not been given. The disturbing thing is that many teachers are unaware of the threats posed for the school's policy makers by national and local initiatives. I have been uncomfortably aware that certain teachers blindly criticise 'the hierarchy' without registering the pressures and burden of administration. Inspection might reveal how defensive this position is. Statements about the hierarchy act as a cover for the speaker's inadequacies. This ploy is often associated with noises about 'being realistic'. The fact may be that the speaker is taking a passive, reactive stance, rather than seeking actively for mastery. Pastoral and academic heads have a responsibility for co-operating to fight such products of stress, caring for their colleagues, helping them master their professional environment. The conflicting goals of sub-populations have to be brought into the open.

Self-evaluation by the various groups helps, provided that Clift *et al*'s (1987) warning is heeded. The fundamental purpose must be improving the quality of experience of teachers and pupils rather than rendering an account. We should look at:

1 The management and use of time. It is striking that the constant emphasis on shortage of time is not accompanied by analysis of usage of time. Whilst time is in inelastic supply, it is still possible to consider whether we use it effectively, and what could be done to ease the pressure on time. (An exercise is included on p. 159.)
2 Evaluation of unintended sources of divisiveness generally in the school, and more specifically amongst the staff. The first is illustrated by the possibility that assemblies, far from reinforcing or expressing corporate identity, function to exacerbate group differences.

3 Analysis of the reasons for misunderstanding of pastoral work, eg 'a shoulder to cry on', and failure to see how it contributes to achievement of educational objectives. Richardson (1973) showed that the basic imagery of the family persisted, perpetuating paternal/maternal role divisions in the school. The helpful incisive analysis by Marland (1983) of gender stereotypy will also illuminate the problem.

4 Territory – psychological and physical – has been touched on. Fears of loss of territory activate irrational opposition and defensive tactics. One version of the problem is the group in which members are bound together by relationships from the past. Mutual commitment of a protective type between members is reinforced by allegiance to some shared and valued experience; the grammar school, the school as it was before amalgamation, or even the previous head whose virtues and wisdom are magnified. Such groups dissociate from current developments: their prime task is to support members against new demands, giving the evasion or resistance apparent legitimacy; increased burdens then fall on others. Should such mechanisms go unchallenged? Harmony in a staff is desirable but the costs may be too great. Pseudo-harmony which masks or denies conflicts of interests is less productive than acknowledging, understanding, and attempting to resolve them.

5 Role clarity and the conflicts produced by ambiguity should be examined. Tutors are not alone in feeling uncertain about how they are assessed. Pastoral heads struggle with the contradictory demands of senior management, academic heads, class teachers, pupils and parents, feeling exposed to unjust and irrational criticisms. For further discussion see Hamblin (1984). The danger is that things will then be done at the wrong level, and heads of year or house undertake what should be the work of the tutor. Senior management then have to provide the detailed management and leadership, or the system lapses into inefficiency.

A concluding note

Integration of the pastoral and curricular demands this simple approach. Heads of house or year must work with academic heads to research the needs and problems of classrooms. I have noticed a curious tendency of enthusiasts to talk as if the pastoral programme influenced classroom behaviours when the needs of the classroom

3 Developing the skills of pastoral heads

The importance of team work

Team work in pastoral activity takes two major forms. First, heads of house or year work as a shared-responsibility team with the appropriate member of the senior management team. Then, on the basis of the support provided by the middle management team, individual year or house heads work with their team of tutors. This statement does not preclude co-operation between heads of year or house in dealing with a group of tutors. The clarification of problems, and the development of common purpose, are an essential prelude to negotiation with academic heads and the action research advocated earlier. In a survey of appraisal schemes HMI (1985) found that appraisal of senior management was not a strong feature of any scheme, whilst no school provided training in interview and appraisal techniques. The same neglect is found in pastoral middle management, but it can be remedied by planned group interaction in which Matza's (1969) appreciative view of behaviour is taken. The focus is not on the behaviour *per se* but on the functions it serves for those who display it. Be warned that such a study can be intimidating. It is possible to think of failure as an achieved status. Pupils achieve it through inappropriate attitudes, lack of skills, and setting peer group values against those of school. Pastoral heads achieve a position of triviality or incompetence by allowing themselves to be swamped by petty tasks, attempting to placate tutors by doing their work for them or colluding with those who hold limited views of pastoral work as 'a shoulder to cry on'. Tough-minded observers might then claim that such behaviour allows pastoral heads to avoid challenge and evade the tasks of managing and leading a team of tutors. Stress then aggravates the situation because the volume of minor administration and trivial tasks increases inexorably. They become caught in a trap from which they see no escape. Analysis of these possibilities is an essential part of developmental team work.

Leadership and team work
King (1984) emphasises two leadership functions which *begin* the development of pastoral heads:

1 Initiating structures, designing, maintaining and improving the system, allowing its members to assist achievement of the purposes of the school.
2 Encouraging and maintaining interlocking cohesive teams, and supporting teachers, so that they commit themselves to the desired outcomes.

Why the *begin*? It calls attention to the fact that these things are scarcely developed in certain schools. Even deputy heads specifically charged with responsibility for the pastoral team perpetuate out-of-date models from earlier decades when pastoral care was seen as requiring little, if any, intellect.

Why this emphasis on team work? All real change involves loss, anxiety and struggle as Fullan (1982) argues. To attempt to avoid uncertainty is to retreat to impotence. Conflict and argument are inevitable but also fundamental to meaningful change. A secure base for pastoral heads in which trust is present, ideas shared critically, support and acceptance readily available is a pre-requisite for development. Fullan's (1982) insightful analysis highlights what was dubbed the Mannheimian approach to truth in Chapter One. Different visions, certainly versions, of the nature of change and its purposes are at work. Pastoral heads who attempt development without deep exploration of these possibilities are undertaking the equivalent of thrusting their bare hands into a hornets' nest: scarcely sensible! The fears, anxieties, misconceptions and honestly held values underlying what we name 'resistance' are rarely studied systematically by pastoral heads.

Gross *et al* (1971) warned about over-reliance on resistance as the explanation for innovatory failure when what was implemented was different to what was intended, perhaps foredoomed to failure. Fullan also argued that the relationship between proclaimed adoption of a change and its actual implementation is uncertain, possibly ambiguous. Adoption without implementation results in a façade, often a paper one, which masquerades as reality. He also (Fullan, 1986) takes up a well-known fact of social psychology (see, for example, Brehm and Cohen, 1962) that attitude change follows rather than precedes behaviour change. Awareness of complexity and complications is therefore not an argument for waiting to initiate action until people are attitudinally ready and intellectually convinced.

Team work amongst pastoral heads, involving co-operation and consequent division of labour, is essential if complexities are to be controlled and tutors given leadership. There is a meaningful distinction between leadership (which requires credibility) and management. Paisey (1984) claims that management is rooted in conformity to the *status quo*; it is more comfortable to manage than lead because risks are fewer and demands less. This reinforces the need for mutual support, and for opportunities to understand the threats and reactions encountered by pastoral leaders. Without it, mild panic may ensue or ill-considered hasty withdrawal from challenges.

A team is gradually built up. The semblance may exist without real co-operation. Equally, we must not confuse the presence of co-operation with the possession of skills. There is much to be learned from looking at a game such as rugby. The captain or team leader occupies the position of first among equals, marked by evidence of skills from past performance, possession of credibility, and the ability to act as a model of competence. He or she (why should a good game be restricted to males?) is acceptable to team members, giving them confidence. When necessary, he/she is able to direct without arousing antagonism. The energies and skills of all team members are fully focused on achievement of the target. A pastoral leader should allow colleagues to define goals; helping them articulate a rationale for their personal development in striving for those goals; providing training tailored to meet the needs of members, identifying and bringing out their potential.

Defence and attack are key elements in team work in games. Constructive attack on problems is salient in a pastoral middle-management team: all too often, we commiserate on the hopelessness of affairs; effectively an endorsement of the *status quo*. It is better to marshal ideas, materials and skills to attack the problem. Anticipatory skills are essential in team games: every team member has to be alert to possibilities; ready to block or assist as necessary. Defence can be under-rated. A team is as good as its defence under attrition or attack! Pastoral defence means clear explanation of pastoral work, dealing with detractors, and forestalling reactions. Certain team members may have special strengths as defenders. Inevitably, a team which ignores the need for vigilant defence is likely to have its good work eroded.

Timing is an essential team work and management skill. The ability to detect the propitious moment for putting proposals is not to be despised; whilst it is obviously inept to initiate training, or make additional demands, at the point of acute pressure. Team members should complement one another's activity. Leaders benefit the whole team by being sensitive to working combinations which are highly productive in particular situations, such as written formulation of policy or training. Against this, power in the team needs debate: if power accrues to one or two members, the unhelpful impact on others may diminish the integrity of the team.

✳ Communication is obviously essential for trust: the effective team leader shares information rather than reserving it to herself or himself. The capacity to explain, detect and bring into the open unvoiced reservations, and accept feedback and criticism, appears obvious, yet it is often absent. Much of the earlier chapters will illuminate this section, but I would urge team members to train themselves to communicate persuasively with staff opinion leaders. As they acquire this skill, they should be evaluating the predictions others are making about the outcomes of team effort, for example 'Wait long enough, and they'll give in, seeing they are getting nowhere'. Attribution of negative intent such as 'empire-building' cannot be ignored. The skill lies in assessing the functions such behaviours serve for their holders, tackling them with energetic good humour and courtesy. To be seduced into diverting effort from the main tasks would be, however, playing their game. Pastoral heads do have to operate in schools where the atmosphere is charged with hostility because morale and self-esteem are generally low. Open communication within the team is crucial to avoid being pushed into paranoid scapegoating. Debate about the form frustrations and challenges are taking, and what happens outside the meetings is not unproductive self-indulgence: it is essential for mental hygiene. Crises of doubt have to be accepted as inevitable, perhaps welcomed as opportunity for further development. Realism also demands the ability to make a constructive temporary 'strategic withdrawal' without its wartime implications of cover for defeat.

Two exercises follow on pastoral team work which have proved useful in various courses.* They should be modified to meet the needs

* *The original documents contained spaces for course members' notes.*

of those using them, and their readiness for tackling the issues. Teachers are forced by pressure and shortage of time to emphasise 'practicality', perhaps undervaluing research and theory. These activities contain theory treated in the traditional way as a system of ideas explaining something. Gibson (1960) points out that 'To have at one's disposal a body of theory . . . is clearly a very great advantage in any enquiry'. Theory, and the associated models, have been largely implicit in pastoral work, although the models of management presented by Bush (1986) merit the attention of pastoral workers.

The team-based skills of heads of year or house

1 The intent of this activity

1.1 To acknowledge the two different aspects of team work:
   (i) Heads of year or house functioning as a mutually supportive and developmental middle management team.
   (ii) Heads of year or house operating with their tutors as a team. (This is dealt with elsewhere.)
1.2 To delineate the skills needed in team work at middle management level.
1.3 To explore the context in which team work occurs, and the way the context shapes outcomes.

2 Your general ideas of team work

2.1 With a partner list the *conditions* that you believe are essential for it to operate effectively.
2.2 Now identify the *skills* necessary to being an effective team member.
2.3 Relate what you have written to the functioning of your group of heads of year or house as a team.

3 The nature of team work
(This will be considered in relation to heads of year or house as a team.)

3.1 A team implies:
   (i) *Leadership*: what is the form that you think it should take?
         Assess the nature of the relationship between the leader and the other team members that you would consider to be desirable.
   (ii) *Division of labour*: what shape and content should this take among the group of year or house heads? Has its presence or absence anything to do with the use of time?
   (iii) *Communication*: what inhibits or facilitates open communication in such teams? What leads to accurate or distorted communication outwards or inwards?
   (iv) *Co-operation*: about what, with whom, and why?

3.2 Now assess the significance of the following statements for possible team work among house or year heads in your school.
   (i) There can be the appearance of a team without any real co-operation existing.
   (ii) We must not confuse the presence of co-operation with the possession of skills.
   (iii) Part of the task of the team of year or house heads is understanding the pressures which keep people immature within the organisation.

4 Your main activity

4.1 Assume you are a middle management team of year or house heads working out a plan for staff development in pastoral care during the next two years.
   (i) State your objectives clearly; break them down into steps which allow implementation to occur whilst the next step is planned.
   (ii) Describe fully the training and other resources that your plan needs.

(iii) Anticipate any resistance or obstacles you think you might meet. Explain how you would circumvent or otherwise deal with them.

(iv) Add other necessary information (the above is merely intended to start you off).

4.2 *Now ask*:

(i) About the timing element. This is an essential management skill. A good team is alert to the appropriate moment and makes full use of it.

(ii) How does one team member complement the activity of another? What partnerships are especially productive within the team? A team leader should be sensitive to combinations which are effective in certain situations.

(iii) Who has well-developed skills in initiating new activities and possesses sufficient credibility to do this? Who has the skills of defending and explaining plans, dealing competently with detractors, and preventing them from belittling initiatives when they are at a vulnerable stage? Middle management teams who ignore the above are likely to have good work eroded.

---

5 Other considerations

5.1 Assess what happens to heads of year or house in your school *outside* their team. Does it constrain, limit or reinforce their pastoral roles?

5.2 What happens *between* team meetings? What forms are frustrations and challenges taking? How does the middle management team deal with them?

5.3 What model of problem-solving activity would you advocate? Would it be a whole group process from the start? Would the problem solving sometimes be delegated to individuals who bring potential solutions back to the team? What other possibilities do you see?

6 Some comments to initiate further discussion

6.1 What rewards are there for the team? We all have needs for affiliation and approval. The pastoral heads' team should produce a climate of acceptance and reward, but is this the case?

6.2 Crises of doubt are inevitable: in fact, they are grist for the team's developmental mill. Doubt can be dealt with rationally, and is part of the team's development. This development itself can be summarised as:

Increasing self-awareness of the team members PLUS growing skills of reading situations accurately, accompanied by knowledge of why, and how, one reacts to and in them, PLUS planned actions based on knowledge of system forces. (The latter includes the value climate of the school, interaction between sub-systems, eg the pastoral and curricular, etc). Unwitting tendencies are included: eg the fact that some pupils in the fourth year are reluctant to see the head of year because 'they only deal with people who are in trouble'.

6.3 Counselling skills are essential for maintaining and extending the team. *List in pairs* the counselling skills you feel are related to team work. Then share ideas, justifying your positions. Finally, summarise your position below.

6.4 It is impossible to examine here the techniques used in the basic counselling stages of:

(i) *Exploration and clarification of the problem*: the initial definition of the problem is not necessarily accurate; system-based and organisational problems often generate defensive smoke-screens which obscure their true nature. Middle management must not accept current definitions of problems without question.

(ii) *The behavioural side* where the problem is dealt with in a systematic way which incorporates flexibility and a step-by-step approach to its resolution.

We can, however, remain aware of them in the group discussions in the training session and in team work within our schools. The general principles of counselling set out below will illuminate the application of counselling skills to pastoral development.

With a *different partner*: examine these general principles of counselling; decide what relevance, if any, they have to effective team work by pastoral heads.

- The counsellor never takes the responsibility away from the person he or she is helping.
- The counsellor tries to look at a situation through the eyes of the other person.
- The task of the counsellor is to help the client understand how she or he defeats herself or himself.
- The counsellor tends to suspend judgements, and is aware of the need to check his or her attributions of motive or intent.
- The counsellor asks, 'What am I making stronger as I work with this person? His sense of competence or inferiority?'
- The counsellor does not condemn, but works to understand what forces people to be aggressive, resort to emotional blackmail or attempt to elicit sympathy.
- The constructive approach is to ask 'What purposes does this behaviour serve for this person?' The counsellor sees this as productive rather than asking the usually unanswerable question, 'Why is he or she like this?'

6.5 Rogers' description of the *characteristics of a helping* relationship is vital. He claims it:
  (i) is accepting and democratic;
  (ii) is based on the perception of the helped that the counsellor trusts him or her;
  (iii) incorporates a feeling of independence, ie that the helped feels he or she is making choices and decisions without pressure or obligation;

(iv) depends on the existence of strong and mutual liking and respect between the counsellor and the helped.

These conditions are necessary for the psychological contact on which counselling rests. Without them, the interaction will be sterile, possibly increasing the difficulties of the client.

Discuss: what is the relevance of these conditions to creating an effective middle-management team?

Perceptions of the nature of man: Rogers' work is not alone in alerting us to the values of the counsellor. McGregor (1960) produces two contrasting theories of the nature of man:

(i) Theory X which is traditional and autocratic. The holder endorses the belief that people must be coerced, directed and strongly controlled. The assumptions are that people prefer direction, want security and avoid responsibility: a passive view of man.

(ii) Theory Y is enlightened and participative. People are seen as exercising self-direction; willing to expend energy in pursuit of goals to which they are committed; and as having the capacity to exercise imagination and ingenuity in pursuit of achievement.

Discuss the likely approach and success of the team leader whose approach to people is that of Theory X.

Management and development of a team of tutors

1 The intent of this activity

1.1 To look for ways of tackling the 'professional learned helplessness' of some tutors which retards development of pastoral activity compared with what is happening in the curriculum.

1.2 To promote a sense of ownership of the pastoral programme, and to stimulate initiative in willing tutors and build the confidence of the uncertain ones.

1.3 To dispel the myth that the head of year or house 'is paid to do pastoral care' when their function is to develop, support and lead a team of tutors.

1.4 To help participants prepare to implement an approach which:

(i) recognises the uniqueness of each school: what works in one school will not necessarily work in another;

(ii) increases tutors' job satisfaction and professional orientation;

(iii) encourages and rewards the initiatives of the tutor.

2 What is the content of the development of the tutor's work?

2.1 Your first step is to outline in concrete terms under appropriate headings what you think the tutor should do.

2.2 Perhaps you ended up with something a little like this:

(i) Monitoring pupils' progress: developing pupils' skills of self-evaluation, target setting and formative assessment.

(ii) Developing tutors' observational skills – training them as 'early warning systems' to note attitudinal, behavioural and other changes.

(iii) Counselling responsibilities etc. But is this precise enough? Examine what you have done. Make it more concrete and build in priorities.

2.3 Now this is fine as far as it goes, but how far has it gone? Has it gone in the right direction? Discuss whether or not this should be done by the tutors themselves. Are tutors almost bound to be passively reactive in many pastoral meetings?

ASK: • Who owns the meeting?
• Who sets the agenda?
• Who has to convince whom?

2.4 Leadership and development may require the head of year to take the position of first among equals. Discuss:
   (i) Is it productive for the year or house head to be the team's sole driving force?
   (ii) Is it important to take keen tutors, allow them to choose the areas of development for which they will take responsibility? They then negotiate with, or train, the year or house team in those areas.
   (iii) How will you employ self-evaluation in the development process? Do you believe it is professionally enhancing for a group to examine openly what they are doing and decide how to tackle the situation?

3 The principles of leading and developing a team of tutors
(Other than those you have already discussed.)

3.1 Identify the principles you would apply in the first year or so of development of your pastoral team from its present position. Arrange them in an order of priority; note also any serious disagreements about importance, order of priority and the reasons for it.

3.2 It may be worth considering the points below:
   (i) It is productive to think in terms of development rather than innovation, which arouses anxiety. New things will be done, but continuity is stressed.
   (ii) Credibility has to be achieved by you as a developer, and for the activities. Some ideas were given in 2 but you need to think more precisely about this.
   (iii) People are suspicious of the leader's capacity – he/she tells us, but can he/she do it? A videotape of you at work is sufficient to break into this – it doesn't have to be perfect!

3.3 Learned professional helplessness is present when teachers develop a 'survival kit' for classroom life to which they adhere rigidly. Abandonment of it appears intolerably threatening. Some tutors do not have the skills of moving from whole class to small group work, perhaps then to partner work, and back to whole class work. These deficiencies can be dealt with through training sessions, but heads of year need to undertake a SKILLS ANALYSIS. Consider the pastoral programme, and *in pairs* work out the skills needed for effective use of:
- role play activities
- decision-making activities
- problem-solving activities.

4 Aspects of leading and developing a team of tutors to which attention should be given by year or house heads in their own INSET

4.1 Decision-making styles. Counselling requires the counsellor to adapt his or her way of working to different individuals, and also to the same individual as he or she progresses. Some will need initial high levels of support and more challenge later. The same is true of leading a group of tutors and the decision-making style of the pastoral middle-management. Bradford and Cohen (1984) see three relevant styles of decision-making:
  (i) *Managerial autonomy*. The manager makes the decision: team members are confined to providing information but they are not encouraged to produce answers, or evaluate what is suggested.
  (ii) *Consultative approaches*. The pastoral head shares the problems with the team using their suggestions and ideas, but he or she still makes the decisions.
  (iii) *Joint decision-making*. Not only are the problems shared with tutors, who generate

ideas, but they make decisions by majority, and also evaluate the results.

Sudden imposition of (iii) would be unrealistic: all three styles have their place. Bion (1961) demonstrated the existence of negative phases and behaviours in therapy groups. We should anticipate them, and not be disorganised or alarmed when they appear as a year or house head attempts to create a shared responsibility group. Some anchorage and stability aids coping: the year head needs to be with his tutors for at least several years; tutors need the rewards and economy of adjustment that come from staying with the same form for as long as possible. As a group, evaluate your decision-making styles as middle managers. If changes are necessary, where will you begin?

4.2 It has been found (Doherty, 1981; Hamblin, 1984) that some teachers see the tutor role as trivial, containing little that is significant. Is it possible that form tutors are professionally under-used? Is the introduction of some form of tutorial programme sufficient to overcome this?

4.3 The next step is that of asking how middle managers in pastoral care try to ensure that tutor work adds to job satisfaction and enhances 'professional self-respect'. Evasion of such difficult questions probably means that pastoral work remains tied to the 'abortive punishment', 'emotional first-aid' or separation of the pastoral and curricular approaches. How would you emphasise the pro-fessional element of pastoral work?

4.4 Bradford and Cohen (1984), in striving to stimulate management for excellence, claim managers should strive to:

   (i) build a shared-responsibility team.
   (ii) continuously develop the individual skills of team members.
   (iii) develop a common vision in the department.

Surely worth considering as the aims of pastoral management? Moreover, even more fundamental is their insistence that *a team achieves excellence by sharing responsibility* for mastering an exciting goal. But what could the goal(s) be for a tutor/pupil team and how will the associated problems be solved? Perhaps it is useful to:

(i) See shared problem-solving as energising, and an opportunity for development.

(ii) Increase pastoral heads' knowledge of group problem-solving techniques. Fox (1987) is amongst those who claim that a small group of concerned and knowledgeable people produce more effective solutions than individuals. Be aware that the influence of the group on its members is diverse and sometimes powerful. A 'risky shift' in decision-making can occur. Fox's methods are worth examining! Rokeach (1960) noted that the dogmatic person tends to pay more attention to the source of the message than its content. Pastoral heads should not allow tutors to confuse the merit of an idea with its source: probationers and 'die-hards' alike can produce fruitful ideas.
Separate sessions are needed for:
- identifying and giving priorities to problems or options
- solving a specific problem.
- making plans for future development.

Now try as a 'group think tank' to resolve the issues below:

(i) Is a pastoral programme necessary but not sufficient to give the larger unifying goals?

(ii) Can you specify unifying goals for each year group which transcend the boundaries of tutor groups? They should challenge and deeply involve pupils and tutors. Contributions to the life of the school should be included, as well as the more usual 'helping' efforts. The targets should be demanding.

(iii) Are there activities/challenges which would unite the curricular with the pastoral? It is vital to find them!

Understanding group interaction

Heads of year or house should have skills which complement those of academic heads. Understanding group interaction, and applying this knowledge in staff development is one such skill. In practice, pastoral heads seem confined to pleasant encouragement and attempts at pacification which end in tutors evading their responsibilities. Yet Argyis *et al* (1984) suggest that over-reliance on praise and minimisation of criticism undermine trust. In this section particular attention will be paid to coping with resistance to change as the context of group interaction.

Ansoff (1984), a distinguished writer on management, shows sensitively, and with precision, the importance of subjective elements in resistance to change. In industry, he shows the impact of the mentality gap through which those successful in the past become sources of resistance or liabilities in an age of change. We must understand teachers whose past success itself acts as a barrier to adaptation to current realities. They feel standards are slipping and that they have little to hope for except early retirement – which will elude them as teacher shortages worsen in the future. We ask them to adapt to active learning and new forms of pastoral activity without understanding the bemusement and desire to regress to an earlier – falsely idyllic – state of affairs which underlies their resistance. Blocks to communication with them have to be removed.

Ansoff claims resistance to change is proportional to the discontinuity brought about by the change, and inversely proportional to the time over which it is spread. Hasty introduction of change creates extra tensions, but there are some individuals who use time to indulge in diatribes and build alliances against change. Ansoff points out that in industry distorted perceptions give rise to more resistance than the facts justify. Pastoral heads as a team have to work out ways of coping with resistance from groups who indulge in delaying tactics, undermining the credibility of the innovation or using sterile arguments as a smoke-screen. Rather than focusing primarily on personality, although it may well play a part, it will be more useful to analyse the situation. Ansoff provides a helpful framework. Groups resist change in proportion to the extent to which it:

1 Threatens their power, privileges and status.
2 Violates the values they take for granted and displaces the norms which shape their interaction with colleagues.

3 Is based on a different view of school life and its purposes than that to which they subscribe.

4 Is justified by information coming from sources regarded as suspect, unreliable or antagonistic.

Team analysis of the reasons for resistance reduces pastoral heads' propensity to blame personality as its cause, and boosts confidence that something can be done. Once the situation is even partially assessed a counter-movement can begin in which anxieties and distortions are tackled, pastoral heads systematically reinforcing their credibility. Sensible use of the mapping technique which identifies the source, nature and intensity of objections removes irresolution. A step-by-step plan can be devised in which the least difficult to resolve behaviours and attitudes are tackled first. Much will be learned in coping with the areas least likely to present acute challenge – especially how to avoid loss of face on both sides. King (1984) argues that middle management should demonstrate its competence by generating useful information, accurately delineating problems and providing realistic solutions. This takes us back to the key skill of reading situations accurately. Achieving this is facilitated by thorough examination by pastoral heads of their beliefs about what will work or will not work in specific situations. They then assess beliefs held by tutors or other colleagues, working out the implications for staff development. Clumsy pressure or crude violation of colleagues' beliefs about what is viable makes them retreat to earlier defensive positions, rejecting attempts at influence. Overcoming resistance is a process initiated by sending messages which fall into the recipients' latitudes of acceptability.

Argyis and Schon (1974) helpfully drew attention to the discrepancy between ideas we claim to hold and those inherent in our actions. What we do is not what we say we do! Part of learning how we defeat ourselves, and how group interaction becomes counter-productive is recognition that 'ideas in action' should be identified, and their consequences evaluated. I run the risk of deluding myself if I ignore this. Unacknowledged emotional blackmail, near disreputable bargaining, setting up evasive smoke screens to evade responsibility or producing guilt in others have to be faced. Year and house heads have to work on these tendencies in themselves, before they can support and develop their tutor teams. Most of us have wondered after a meeting what individuals were *not* saying. Heads of year should explore as a team the thoughts they keep to themselves in their own meetings, senior management meetings they attend, meetings with academic heads or tutors. This could be followed by exploration of selective tendencies in listening. Is there a selective process at work which allows one to dismiss the speaker, or do we listen to prove him or her wrong or inadequate?

As teachers we are better known by what we do in the classroom than by our alleged subscription to the values of child-centredness, active learning or caring. Theories in use have different purposes from those their holder recognises: others infer those purposes from our actions. I have found the slightly modified exercise based on Argyis and Schon (1974) which is set out below to be highly productive in training.

(There is, however, no substitute for reading Argyis *et al* (1984) which could be of immense value to the pastoral team.)

---

1 Describe briefly a challenging interview or incident which has occurred this term.
2 Outline your purposes. Describe the other person or persons and the setting in which the event took place.
3 Now briefly outline the ways in which you dealt with it, and how you hoped to achieve your ends.
4 Now turn the situation into a somewhat unusual playlet.
   The crucial instructions are:
   (i) On the left-hand side write what you and the other person said or did, strictly in the order in which it happened.
   (ii) On the right-hand side write what was going on in *your* mind as the other person or you spoke or acted.
   (iii) *Always comment on your thoughts immediately after entering each action or statement on the left-hand side.*

Person	What was said or done	What was going on in your mind

5 Assess the validity of your assumptions about effective action in this situation. Look at your behaviours. List them below. What was their purpose, eg implicit threat or coaxing agreement with your point of view?

The Incident Analysis (Hamblin, 1984, p. 230) has also been useful in stimulating awareness of less obvious features of interaction, such as awareness of the hidden audience whose later judgements shape behaviours, perceptions of the motives of participants and beliefs about authority. Both approaches help people discover how they unwittingly deceive themselves.

The existence of Machiavellian power tactics in which a colleague manipulates others for his or her own ends is uncomfortable to acknowledge in a caring profession. Pastoral heads are sometimes unwilling to admit they have colleagues who have a utilitarian view of interaction which stresses the pay-off for them. Goffman's (1959) cool, calculated manager of impressions and Christie and Geis's Machiavellian may be encouraged by the ambiguities and doubt produced by ill-understood change. These individuals are suspicious of others, interpreting events and motives cynically. This is more than the embitterment stemming from redeployment or blocked promotion: it is a deep-seated orientation towards manipulation in social and professional interaction. Alertness is essential, for the Machiavellian works to keep his manipulation from becoming obvious: to be visible is to be ineffective. Pastoral heads are often at a disadvantage in coping with the Machiavellian because they are likely to become involved, letting their concern for the needs of others influence their actions. This is then exploited. Distasteful as the Machiavellians' behaviour is, we can still learn from them. They have, according to Christie and Geis (1970), the skills of processing information thoroughly, and detecting advantageous routes to goals. These are skills pastoral heads can develop without adopting the Machiavellian's orientations. (Machiavellianism will be discussed later in connection with staff appraisal.)

This may be an appropriate point at which to raise the need for deep consideration of the ethics of pastoral work. What are the justifications for, and limits to, intervention? Is there a place for confidentiality in pastoral work? If so, what burdens does this place on pastoral heads? Does pastoral concern impinge on the freedom of the individual or foist negative identities on them? Is the caring proffered an inadequate attempt at compensating for organisational defects? Does it give pupils support with the hidden costs of accepting the identity of a 'problem pupil'? Is it possible that the pastoral system functions over the years to strengthen dependency and erode initiative and enterprise? Equally important questions have to be answered about colleagues. What are the limits of loyalty to them? If someone is severely stressed or working against the policies of the school what must be done? To neglect these issues is to lay a minefield into which we unthinkingly stumble.

Chapter One highlighted the need for analysis between sub-groups in the school. Pastoral heads have to equip themselves to analyse and facilitate change. Lewin pointedly said the best way of understanding the world is to try and change it. But ill-prepared and under-equipped forays into change may force retreat from the attempt baffled, hurt and humiliated. One of the most promising sets of tools comes from 'action science' as developed by Argyis *et al* (1985) who cited Lewin. I shall not attempt to summarise the techniques: certainly I cannot do credit to the thought and research. Heads of year or house must investigate action science for themselves.

Action science is engagement in a 'collaborative process of critical enquiry'. It is a form of action research involving exploration of significant problems in their setting. Heads of year or house as a group should grapple with the hidden significance of their daily work and its problems. The 'hidden significance' indicates that the process takes place over a considerable period, and involves cycles of identification of its facets, evolving strategies for tackling it, acting on them and evaluation. One thinks in terms of layers of the problem situation, and gradual emergence of meaning, rather than a neat, immediate and probably deceptive solution to it. Pastoral heads using action science approaches must be prepared to train themselves to generate alternative explanations and challenge existing data. There are two levels of investigation corresponding to theories in use and theories espoused. The first requires investigation and decision-making concerned with the means available to reach a particular goal. The second identifies, and then chooses between, competing perspectives and values. The importance of the value climate or culture of the school was remarked on in the previous chapter. Change may rest on understanding of the values expressed in interaction between individuals or groups. The emphasis in action research is on values, and the meaning of patterns of behaviour related to them. This is not unique to action research for Ansoff (1984), Fullan (1982), Holly (1986; 1987) and Parlett and Hamilton (1972) all stress in their various ways the importance of comprehending the meanings of behaviour and change. Significance gradually emerges: meaning which seems obvious is found to have latent aspects and functions; it varies with the context, therefore the same behaviours or values carry vastly different connotations. We have seen that the intent of people may not be what they claim it is, so it would be foolish to take it for granted. Speculation about intent will be rewarding, although the evidence must be assessed.

Heads of year or house must apply intellectual discipline to their developmental tasks. As a team, pastoral heads should set out to develop their skills of critical thinking. This is more than criticism: it is the capacity to appraise objectively the strengths and weaknesses of argument or research. The work of Watson and Glaser (1964) and Ausubel (1968) amongst others allows one to identify five basic skills. Weinstein *et al* (1988) (eds) also helpfully examine strategies in learning. The skills are:

1 The ability to define a problem accurately, detecting its dimensions. Obviously a false initial definition of a problem handicaps the thinker. Yet problem solving often flounders because the nature of the problem was taken for granted.
2 The ability to select relevant information. A number of sub-skills are involved, eg
  • scanning which is directed towards distinguishing between salient and marginal elements;
  • analysis which breaks the problem down into its elements;
  • questioning particularly directed at detection of *unstated* assumptions.
3 The ability to formulate, and then test in some way, relevant hypotheses. The suppositional nature of a hypothesis, ie 'If this, then under these conditions, this probably follows' must be kept in mind. It has to be submitted to rational scrutiny, and validated practically.
4 To use means/end thinking in working out the steps to a solution. (It is sometimes productive to work backward from the goal to the problem situation.)
5 The ability to draw conclusions validly, and to judge the soundness and defensibility of your inferences.

Pastoral heads who are taking their developmental role seriously cannot afford to impose instant meanings on situations, closing their minds and refusing to admit further evidence. Neither can they allow the credibility of arguments to be determined by their source rather than the content. Causality cannot be taken for granted. Hume, long ago, pointed out that because Event A is habitually followed by Event B it is all too easy to assume that a causal relationship exists, when it may merely be contiguity in time and/or space. Over-simple notions of causality have to be questioned, especially the tendency to believe in *the* cause, which is denial of the complexity of social situations. False assumptions of similarity with, or difference from previous situations is unhelpful; group discussion then becomes anecdotal rather than analytic, sliding into cosy irrelevance.

Argyis *et al* argue that problem solving incorporates key processes of *naming* and *framing*. Within the group we name that to which we will attend, giving those things salience and emotive significance as good or bad etc. We also frame the context in which this occurs. Heads of department may frame a staff or other meeting as a situation in which they show publicly that they are prepared to fight for the best possible deal for their department in the face of others' opposition. At this juncture, pastoral heads would benefit from discussing the *naming* and *framing* occurring in the meetings they attend or organise. Standpoint-taking implies understanding the *naming* and *framing* operating in participants. What are the implications of discrepancies for future co-operation and development? Development undertaken without these, and other considerations, invites the growth of resistance in which group members collude to produce shared justifications for condemning proposals. This respectable front may hide rather nasty feelings about the motives of those sponsoring the change. Statements then differ from the underlying reality of action.

This commonsense approach means assessment of the direct and covert anxiety in interaction between colleagues, with pupils, or in coping with innovation, accepting that it can be disguised as intolerance, confidence or superiority or give rise to aggression. Anxiety, its manifestations and consequences, is worthy of more intensive study than it receives in the secondary school. Without condoning it, the reasons for minimal or superficial performance in pastoral work should be studied; they may lie, for example, in feelings of being 'passed over' unjustly in the promotion race, or of being ignored and unable to influence the course of events. Discussion of these matters, initially at middle-management level, eventually between a pastoral head and tutor team, is part of caring for the carers. It should be part of the professional support to which the teacher is entitled, allowing him or her to cope with stress and use their skills to the full. (The links with staff appraisal of a constructive type are fairly obvious.) We all constantly scan our social environment, evaluating ourselves, using the performance of others as a basis for comparison. Some unrealistically see themselves as failures, whilst some deny the authenticity of signals which indicate their incompetence. Defensive denials of criticism pose problems, but the most difficult to support are colleagues who depress themselves by pessimistic, harsh comparisons: they dispirit the helper.

As they work to improve their understanding pastoral heads will become aware that system-based troubles generate false explanations which frequently insinuate that a particular group, for example senior management or tutors, are at fault. Invitations to such scapegoating have to be rejected instantly. It is important to focus on behaviours individuals use, but we have to see them, not invent them. In full-time training of counsellors I had to help them work through a pseudo-Freudian stage of easy explanation of their clients' behaviours – Freudians would, of course, have been the first to reject such loose conceptualisation. Yet action research calls attention to the need to look for projection ie attributing what we do not or cannot recognise in ourselves to others. Someone concentrates on a colleague's alleged aggression – because of this, they then behave towards him or her in ways which call out aggression. Then they take that expression of aggression as confirmation of their original attribution of an aggressive personality. Circular patterns of behaviour such as this have to be studied because they form a greater part of group interaction than most people realise.

Proposed and implemented change often activates variants of the defensive behaviours below:

1 *Rationalisation* or the inventing of reasons for behaviours after they have occurred. It is unhelpful, not only because it is obscurant, but because it provides no guidelines for action, wastes time, and, when examined closely, is usually hidden blaming of others.
2 *Reaction-formation* which is a form of protesting too much. Exaggeration of the soundness of past and current practices, and of the potential dangers of the proposed developments are its most common form.

3 *Denial* of the need for change and the validity of the data or arguments supporting it. Note that the denial is irrational, the individual obdurately refuses to consider the evidence.
4 *Displacement* where aggression, opposition and blame are expressed but are directed towards people who are not responsible or unable to protest.

Argyis *et al* (1984) in their exposition of action science comment that face-saving and covert evaluations bring sterility. The behaviours outlined above are futile, preventing helpful examination of problems. Pastoral heads would benefit from the helpful analysis of protective strategies which exacerbate problems, and stultify development under the guise of being supportive. Action science spurs one to understand events, then builds awareness of what can be done to induce positive change. I commend it to pastoral heads who are seeking better ways of coping and wish to construct new pathways into the future. I stress that in no way have I offered a full exposition of what is a valuable tool for organisational development.

Simple problem-solving activities

1 The rationale behind the approach

1.1 'Simple' topics are raised, which you are asked to relate to your experience and situation, examining its implications in depth.

1.2 It is hoped that this will be more meaningful than giving detailed situations or problems to be 'solved'. I have done this, but have wondered if there has been any transfer of skill from the artificial to the 'real life' of individuals.

1.3 The topics are:
   (i)   crises;
   (ii) resistances;
   (iii) things being done at the wrong level;
   (iv) self-defeating behaviours.

2 Crises

2.1 Some pastoral systems, if they are systems, seem to focus on crises.

    (i) Give, and justify, your definition of a crisis.

    (ii) Heads of year or house in some schools are frequently called on to leave their classes and deal with crises by colleagues; but what concept of a crisis is held by their colleagues? How does it/they compare with that held by the head of year or house?

2.2 Is the concept of crisis:

    (i) Reflecting something important about heads of year or house's conceptions of their role? Do these conceptions need to be clarified, perhaps challenged?

    (ii) Saying something about the beliefs of others about:

- the limits of their responsibilities;
- the task of the year or house head?

2.3 If the concept of 'crisis' is being misused in your school how would you approach the problem of change? (Never forget the importance of consumer research. How do the students, often at the centre of the crisis, view it, and how would they react to the proposed changes?)

2.4 Assess the impact on the roles of others that your change would make. How would you ensure that tutors and teachers could cope? What part would heads of academic departments play?

2.5 Would there be a gradual return to the former state of affairs? How would this be anticipated and prevented?

A general note:

Your work on 'crises' may have alerted you to the power of *expectations*: they are individual or shared beliefs about what are proper attitudes and actions for a person in a particular role. Shared expectations may operate to make certain behaviours habitual and unquestioned. Attempts at changing them, or the mere suggestion of change, provoke resentment and resistance. Middle managers in pastoral care have to be prepared to analyse this resistance and employ appropriate strategies for working through it.

3 Resistance to change and development

3.1 Resistance/opposition is a source of tension for many heads of year or house, yet they do not seem to have a relevant *shared* plan for tackling it. Some wait for the resistance to disappear, some wait for a revelatory prophet to appear, some wait for a simple recipe to be presented that will change things, and some just wait!

3.2 Pastoral managers should not condemn those who resist, nor should they restrict their explanations to 'personality'. They should use their capacity for standpoint-taking to look at the changes through the eyes of the 'resisters'. They will then be sensitive to the meaning of the changes for those resisting them.

3.3 Ask about a group or an individual resisting pastoral change in your school:

(i) Is their behaviour a product of lack of knowledge, or misunderstanding of the purposes of pastoral work, and especially the new development.

(ii) Is it the habitual response of a disaffected person to anything new?

(iii) What justifications do the individual or group proffer for their resistance? Do you think it is based in deep conviction or is it merely defensive or after-the-event justification?

(iv) Is the resistance that of those who have been successful in the past, but who have found that yesterday's remedies are no longer effective, but cannot accept it?

These are illustrations only, and not exhaustive. Each requires a different approach. Work out how you would deal with the resistances you meet – an initial outline only.

3.4 Sensible questions to ask *when you have some idea of the dimensions of the problem*:

(i) Is the resistance a reaction to insecurity? Is threat involved, eg the feeling that new teaching skills are demanded, and the person(s) feel he/she/they will be inadequate? But beware loose resort to such explanations: they are too easy. What is your evidence?

(ii) Have changes in power and status recently occurred which created resentment? Is the resistance a statement of resentment about this or a form of displaced, indirect aggression?

(iii) Are games being played? An example: the appearance of co-operation, coupled with constant procrastination accompanied by 'good' reasons?

Construct a resistance map related to your school. It may take any form that is meaningful to you.

Resistance is supported by irrational justifications for it and distorted beliefs about the nature of the changes.

Work out your step-by-step plan for eliminating exaggerations, distortions and coping with rumour. How will you use opinion leaders positively?

3.5 Wider considerations for pastoral management discussions:

(i) Resistance can be realistic or unrealistic. The former is based on difficulties actually existing: the latter is an irrational response to tensions and long-standing grievances within the school.

(ii) Unrealistic resistance may stem from accumulated resentments about earlier poor management or injustices. Suspicion of the intent of developments then takes aggravated forms and undermines sound development. (Some new heads have to face this as part of the legacy from an earlier regime.)

---

4 Things **being** done at the 'wrong level'

4.1 This may well be a major source of inefficiency and tension. Senior management who undertake the work of heads of year or house are going to feel stress. Heads of year or house who attempt to placate form tutors by removing work from them or who do their work for them are going to remain at a low level of competence and find themselves exhausted.

4.2 ASK:
(i) What is it that instigates and maintains the situation where things are done at the wrong level?
(ii) What *should be done* at each level? (A starter idea is given for each level.)
Deputy head(s): Provide skills which allow pastoral heads to function as a middle-management team.
Pastoral head(s): Leading and training a team of tutors.
Tutors: Giving initial help and counselling which meets the needs of most pupils:

4.3 Now identify key elements which help to ensure things are dealt with at the right level, eg tutors knowing which difficulties they must deal with, and which ones should be referred to the year or house head.
Make notes on:
(i) the steps that will have to be taken in your school;
(ii) the difficulties you anticipate, *and* the evidence for their existence;
(iii) the order in which you will tackle the steps, giving your reasons.

5 Self-defeating behaviours

Perls, in the Gestalt approach to counselling, argued that the counsellor should help the client to discover how he/she defeats himself or herself. This is relevant for the manager. A keen eye for self-defeating behaviours, followed by effective modification of behaviour, is one of the elements of creative management.

5.1 Here are a few examples of self-defeating behaviours noted by Hamblin (1984):
  (i) Heads of year or house complaining that tutors will not take their role seriously, whilst simultaneously telling pupils that if they have a problem they should come straight to them, the head of year or house.
  (ii) Allowing the situation to develop in which creative teachers feel relationships with pupils are damaged because they are required to track down miscreants as their major function. They then reject the tutor role.
  (iii) Talking about caring and responsibility but not adjusting methods to pupils' ages and needs. Therefore the fifth year methods differ little from those used in the first year.
  (iv) Not seeing that we are *not* stimulating initiative and *not* giving opportunities for responsibility in pastoral activity.
5.2 Find examples of self-defeating practices in your pastoral system. List them below, making suggestions for remedying them.
5.3 Now take the standpoints of fifth year students in your school. Give what you believe would be their views of the nature, purpose and effectiveness of pastoral activity.
  (i) Summarise the viewpoints
     (If you believe sub-populations have different views, report them separately.)
  (ii) Comment on the significance of fifth year viewpoints. Do they, in any way, illuminate self-defeating forces? If differences between pupil

> sub-groups appear to exist, what does this mean? Is it self-defeating to ignore such differences, including the different developmental rates of the sexes?

Resolution of staff conflict

Jones (1987) in her challenging discussion of school leadership, indicates that heads are often uneasy about their competence as negotiators and resolvers of staff conflict. Startlingly, pastoral heads who should have an integrative function for the school, give little evidence that they see conflict resolution skills as a key element in their expertise. Divisiveness and diffusion of energy are perpetuated by this omission. A first step is assessment of the nature and functions of conflicts which undermine productive relationships. Conflicts in school seem to spring from:

1 *Breaches and protection of territory*. Teachers are sensitised early in their careers to the importance of physical and psychological domains and become vigilant in their protection.
2 *Priorities*, especially those concerned with the status of both the individual and a department.
3 *Changes in role* where loss of face and reduction of the role-holder's sphere of influence seem inevitable.
4 *New demands* for which individuals are ill-equipped, and where the justifications for those demands appear illegitimate.
5 *Fear of loss of credibility* in the eyes of colleagues.

Having delineated the nature of conflicts in the school, the team of pastoral heads should ask when conflict is likely to escalate. They should be working to prevent those conditions from appearing. Guidelines are provided by Deutsch's (1973) monumental work. Conflict grows when the incentive to win is strong; fear of loss of face, anxiety and refusal to listen to others' viewpoints make communication erratic, tense and provocative. Subtle diplomacy is prime in preventing colleagues committing themselves publicly to a position; for change of opinion means appearing inconsistent. Pastoral heads have to keep interaction open by applying their counselling skills of constructive listening and sending signals of acceptance as the beginning of negotiation. Simulations of negotiations based on the conflicts discovered and the likely reactions of colleagues provide realistic preparation. The more, the better! Sensitivity in negotiation is essential, and takes at least two forms: alertness to past actions or positions from which the individual or group cannot escape without humiliation or rebuff; recognition as Argyis *et al* (1985) argue, that to call someone insensitive or inadequate is to be that oneself.

Conflict between groups keeps each group together, sharpening its boundaries, and giving its members a sense of belonging. In schools, we have the situation where each group honestly sees its motives and behaviours as more benevolent, ethical and professional than the other. The old point that no conflict is more radical than that pursued with a good conscience obtains! Unless problem-solving communication is established and maintained, both sides produce new justifications for their positions, clinging more determinedly to them. Conflict *within* a group can be understood through Coser's (1965) reformulation of Simmel's propositions. He talks, for example, of the heretic who finds alternative pathways of action where others want none to exist, or the renegade who becomes the focus of hostility because he has abandoned the values of the group. Individual counselling may be necessary to help the individual trapped in such roles, but we also need to deepen understanding of group behaviours. (For this, the work of Napier and Gershenfeld (1973) provides a sound introduction for middle management.)

Little wonder that heads saw conflict resolution as requiring more training! Pastoral heads have to see how black and white thinkers generate conflicts. These individuals impose instant meaning on the responses of others, rejecting further information which would modify their perceptions. Some protagonists cannot accept that their justifications for past actions are faulty. Not only must such possibilities be considered, but pastoral heads must take into account the context in which conflict occurs. Redeployment, falling rolls, or a change of headmaster or headmistress, may be significant. With the departure of an autocratic head previously suppressed conflicts emerge, exacerbated by suspicion of the 'real motives' of the more democratic new incumbent. Dependencies had been created, but in the new regime responsibility is demanded, creating unwillingness and defensive behaviours.

Pastoral heads coping with conflict should:

1 Avoid trapping themselves in unproductive analysis, eg if they focus on personality rather than behaviours, they make themselves helpless.

2 Have a proper awareness that a hidden agenda probably exists. They learn to ask, 'What purposes does this conflict serve? Are they what they appear to be at first sight?' They then question their evidence critically. The rush of school life pushes us into over-simplification. We saw in Chapter One that sub-populations in the school have versions of 'truth' which allow them to disparage others, resist influence or see themselves as the victims of 'hierarchy's' inefficiency or machinations.

3 Employ the counselling skill of *confrontation*. This is not aggressive, nor does it contradict earlier statements about threat avoidance. It is about the productive exploration of discrepancies and distortions in the rationale which justifies conflict. The intent is to ask for elucidation in order to understand. Too often, neither side has correctly apprehended the other's perspective. Pressure is avoided by sending signals of respect; to do otherwise polarises positions, hardens attitudes and prevents unfreezing.

Let us now look at negotiation in conflict situations a little more closely.

The tensions produced by what seem to be never-ending changes make us long for harmony, but its price is too high if it stifles enterprise and originality. As we examine conflict resolution we should be clear that not every conflict is pernicious: some facilitate development by sharpening issues helpfully.

The first step for pastoral heads attempting conflict resolution is to obtain illumination from studying previous conflicts in the school or college. What seemed to bring them into being? What sharpened them? How were they resolved, and did the resolution give rise to new, possibly more intractable problems? Carpenter and Kennedy (1988) state that ignorance about the genesis and course of conflicts leads to inaccurate assumptions about the motivation of contesting parties, and unintended trampling on strongly held values. They warn that one should never attempt to negotiate on the basis of values: asking people to revise their values is trying to get them to revise their 'sense of reality'.

Suspicion and anxiety are strong in conflicts. Long-standing frustrations and irritations bring distrust to the point where the consequences of statements and action are disregarded. Therefore negotiators have to think deeply: the lid can be taken off but can it be replaced? If not, credibility will then be diminished; whilst the inadequate tactics bring hostility to bear on the mediators.

Negotiators have to establish impartiality within the clearly bounded areas of the conflict. Any hint of bias renders negotiation almost impossible, whilst the battle to win gains legitimacy. This alone is enough to make pastoral heads question their capacity as negotiators. As values cannot be made the issue, the first step is to get the parties to agree on a shared definition of the problem. Easily said: achieved with difficulty! Participants readily claim that their interests are being neglected, forcing pastoral heads towards a defensive position. Counselling skills of anticipating difficulties and desensitising situations by statements which signal empathy, such as 'It seems very difficult for you not to feel . . .', or 'From your viewpoint it must be . . .' are essential to maintain communication. If legitimacy is denied to perceptions, then their possessors cling to them more strenuously.

Choice – another basic element in counselling – has to be built into negotiation. A range of possibilities has to be developed by participants. The negotiator's task is to clarify them to prevent people believing that they agreed to something different from what was intended. Systematic elucidation of the viewpoints of the proponents is obviously necessary, yet in practice this is a haphazard activity. Participants have a right to be able to confirm that the negotiator has an accurate understanding of their perspectives.

Let us look more closely at the basic conditions for negotiation. Coopersmith (1967) pointed out that for the growth of self-esteem and positive attitudes to others, children require firm boundaries within which there is freedom for initiative and experiment. It is interesting that this is exactly what is required for conflict resolution. With the firm boundaries go ground rules which have to be maintained resolutely as conflict is explored. Carpenter and Kennedy stress that ground rules have to be negotiated, but once established, they must be adhered to. One extremely useful ground rule might be that individuals must not recite past grievances, but deal with the 'here and now'.

A process of problem solving is therefore initiated in which the parties proffer solutions. Heads of year or house will, as negotiators, discipline themselves to remain neutral and not express preferences, unless they want to meet later accusations and become defensive. They clarify, calling attention to neglected questions, but in recapitulating the strengths and weaknesses of a proposal they guard against wandering into territory where they could lose credibility.

The silent member has to be considered: in a grave conflict

situation brought my way recently, I found that the dangerous, manipulative person was silent in staff meetings, but was active afterwards destructively and indirectly. Silent members may be such because they see it as helpful; it may be a ploy for gaining attention and thus bolstering their power; alternatively, they may have nothing to say. Negotiators note changes in the pattern of interaction, such as somebody initially vociferous who becomes silent, or the reverse. They then assess the reasons. If the silent person feels unable to voice reservations, she or he will implement group decisions half-heartedly.

Negotiators should have a sharp eye for processes and methods, judging when it is productive to break into small groups, brainstorm, or allocate deeper investigation of part of a problem to a sub-group. Agreement to leave a tricky area for a future meeting may need to be gained; but only the negotiator whose probity is accepted is able to do this.

The basic rule in conflict resolution is to take nothing for granted, and never be surprised if your motives are questioned. Agreement to a course of action is never total; some endorse but are cynical about outcomes and others' motives for putting the proposal forward. A troubled area is follow-up between meetings. Misunderstandings may compel some action after the meeting, but it must be done openly and explained if accusations of manipulation and attempted politicising are not to reactivate suspended distrust. The skill needed is that of listening to implicit meanings without assuming that one's interpretations are necessarily correct. Alertness to what could be said – what the person seemed likely to say, but did not, is crucial. We tend to doubt claims of honesty, but the skill lies in knowing when such phrases as 'frankly speaking' are fraudulent, void of meaning, or indicate what is happening.

Conflict brings the determination to prove that one's own side is right and the other view misguided. As they engage in interaction, people will discard their rigid views, but it is easy to forget that they will be hypersensitive to even faint signals of devaluation. Negotiators do have the power to attack or put down, but effective negotiators are aware that this, and other forms of power, tend to lose potency if used. Attention given to the meaning of interaction aids resolution of conflict. Even if the desire for resolution is genuine, people remain frozen into old networks of relationships and patterns of behaviour. Resolution means facilitation of awareness of the costs and rewards of such interaction. Lieberman *et al* (1973) in studies of effective therapeutic group leadership showed the importance of attribution of meaning to individual and group behaviour. As 'interpreters of reality' they focus attention on group climate and working habits, inviting reflection on what has been taken for granted. Factions and unhelpful pairing of individuals have to be brought into the open. Personal attacks have to be stopped immediately as breach of the ground rules.

Negotiators, like counsellors, are sensitive to key images and symbols. They recognise that for an individual or group, phrases exist which trigger off immediate deep and complex reactions. Phrases or images of this kind condense many meanings and are highly emotive. They should be avoided by the negotiator unless she or he is very skilled – when they can be used therapeutically. For the rest of us, avoidance must be the maxim.

Flexibility in devising solutions is essential: that means treating them as possibilities liable to revision. Prescriptions are futile, but one works to take the risk of loss of face out of proposed solutions. Beyond this there *are* no recipes. A simple exercise allows discussion of some of these points.

Problem-solving activity related to conflict resolution

1 The background to this aspect of management

1.1 Jones (1987) reports that a number of heads feel ill-prepared to cope with the resolution of conflicts that inevitably arise in a large school, especially during a period in which individuals feel over-whelmed by change.

1.2 Coping with conflicts, managing them, and some-times anticipating them, is part of the work of heads of year or house operating as a team. Problem-solving activity is involved: as a first step it will be useful for you to state what you
  (i) mean by problem solving;
  (ii) consider to be the skills involved.

1.3 Cognitive skills are as important as interpersonal ones in problem solving (Rose and Edleson, 1987). They include:
  (i) the capacity for *alternative thinking*, ie the ability to generate multiple solutions.

(ii) *consequential thinking*, ie the ability to anticipate accurately *in a particular context* the
short-run and long-run consequences of
alternative courses of action.

(iii) *means–end thinking* or the ability to plan a
series of specific actions essential to reaching
the desired solution: this includes recognition
of obstacles and a realistic time framework.

Now work out the elements and stages in a model
of problem solving that is meaningful to you.

1.4 Look at the situations of conflict you meet in your
professional work. How do you cope? What short-
run and long-run costs are attached to the coping?

---

2 Looking at conflict in your school

2.1 *Map out* the sources and types of conflict in your
school. Distinguish between:

(i) those that need to be dealt with and those
which can be tolerated or even have a positive
function.

(ii) those related to pastoral work; those not based
in pastoral work but which impinge on it; those
which seem not to be your concern.

Also comment on the functions of the conflicts you
see as especially important to pastoral work. Share
ideas in the group.

2.2 Take one conflict and engage in a group problem-
solving exercise about *ways* of resolving it.

(i) Succinctly give the dimensions of the conflict.

(ii) Generate as many approaches to tackling the
problem as possible.

(iii) What snags do you anticipate? How would you
cope with them?

2.3 The pastoral management team must learn to
anticipate conflict; to intervene at an early stage in
a positive way, taking note of low level signals of
tension or dissatisfaction. Discuss how you will
work as a team on this.

3 Recognising conflict

3.1 Ansoff (1984) in discussing industry talks about 'mentality filters' which prevent managers from seeing incipient conflicts and lead them to ignore signals of tension because they were not significant in the past. What new sources of conflict arise in this era of rapid educational change? How can pastoral middle management train themselves in the skills of recognising incipient conflicts and positive intervention?

3.2 Conflict can appear between:
  (i) the school and a parent;
  (ii) a pupil and a teacher;
  (iii) a tutor and a head of year or house;
  (iv) a head of year or house and head of an academic department.

Take *one* and:
  (i) describe the nature of the conflict;
  (ii) look more closely at its functions, using the information given earlier;
  (iii) work out possible *ways* of resolving the conflict;
  (iv) submit your solution to the group for appraisal.

Pastoral meetings

Pastoral meetings may alienate, produce boredom, or convince those who are unsure that there is little point in pastoral work. It would therefore be sensible for one head of year or house to acquire some academically sound knowledge of groups, passing this on to her or his colleagues. The exercise below has proved useful in training groups.

Effective pastoral meetings

The purpose of this activity

1 To help pastoral heads examine the nature of communication and interaction in pastoral meetings, including those held by the senior management for the pastoral heads.

2 To assess latent processes at work in these meetings and consider whether 'hidden agendas' are at work.

3 To consider the techniques that can be used to make such meetings become more productive: they do not have to be counter-productive or only marginally useful.

STEP ONE: An overview of attitudes and behaviour

1 Assess the strengths of your pastoral meetings with tutors. What makes them satisfying for *you* and for *other participants*? Note any differences carefully.

1.1 Standpoint-taking is a key element on which effective management is based. Take a person who seems to regard the pastoral meetings negatively, eg as an imposition, irrelevant, or an example of empire building. Write a brief description of the meeting from their point of view. Now do the same with a positive member. *Compare the two positions*, discussing the implications for your future behaviours in the meetings.

1.2 Identify themes that are frequently present, eg
Obviously negative ones
   • insufficient time
   • futility of pastoral activity
Misconceptions
   • pastoral work is about 'giving them a shoulder to cry on'
   • it is the head of year's task to provide pastoral care
Positive perceptions
   • tutor periods allow the tutor to make better relationships with a group of pupils
   • tutor work contributes to good discipline
ASK:
   (i) What purposes do these themes serve for those who raise them? Do not assume that the apparently positive is such. People may say nice things to avoid questioning and challenge.

(ii) How are they tackled? Why do we not look more closely and critically at issues such as time or tackle limited ideas about pastoral care?

STEP TWO: Analysis of structure and roles

2 Some awareness of the patterns of communication in meetings has probably been acquired if Step One was undertaken thoroughly. Roles in meetings tend to be taken up in more or less the same way by the same individuals. Others begin to expect this of them, anticipating, and even fostering, the occupation of these roles, eg the resident cynic, the time waster.

2.1 Map your pastoral meeting(s) in terms of the roles that people take up. Following Bales (1970) you could assess their:
  (i) *Power* in the group – do they tend to be dominant or passively acquiescent?
  (ii) *Impact on others* – do they arouse positive feelings or create tensions?
  (iii) *Contribution to the work of the group* – do they foster or retard achievement of the work objectives?
  (The above is based on Bales' approach but does not replicate it exactly.)
2.2 Next look for patterns of interaction. Structure is habitual patterns of behaviour accompanied by expectations and rewards or sanctions from others. ASK:
  (i) Do certain individuals 'pair up', offering support to one another against others or the group task?
  (ii) Who communicates with whom?
  (iii) Who is listened to, and who is disregarded?
  (iv) Whose ideas are taken up, and acted on, and whose ideas are rejected?
  (v) To whom, if to anybody, do people refer ideas for appraisal or comment?

(vi) With whom do you seem to interact? In what way?

2.3 Discuss the significance of this analysis to your attempts at staff development. What can you build on? As a middle manager have you seen the importance of studying group interaction in this way?

STEP THREE: The mechanisms operating in pastoral meetings

3 Managerial skills include recognition of, and dealing with, the ways people cope with real or imagined threat in group situations, subvert the purposes of the meeting, or defend themselves against change.

3.1 Try to find examples of, and describe to your fellow trainers:
   (i) A person setting up a smoke-screen to distract attention away from his real purposes.
   (ii) Someone exaggerating, probably without concrete evidence, the alleged dangers of a proposed development in pastoral work.
   (iii) The tactics of devaluation, eg making accusations of 'empire building', or otherwise decrying the integrity of the pastoral head.
   (iv) Black and white thinking, where instant meaning is imposed on a situation, and the person then resolutely refuses to consider other evidence.
   (v) Passive resistance.
   (vi) Denial that a problem or problems exist.
   (vii) The person who makes destructive remarks at the end of the meeting where they cannot be dealt with.

3.2 NOW:
   (i) Look at your tutor group or fellow pastoral heads and list the mechanisms they employ that give you concern.

> (ii) Take one and work out a way of coping with it constructively.
>
> (iii) Share your ideas in your small training group offering appraisal of ideas for coping and supportive suggestions.

STEP FOUR: Working out a plan for improving pastoral meetings

4 Analysis can become inertia; action without analysis is blind. On the basis of the examination it should be possible to make plans for improving the productivity of your pastoral meetings.

4.1 Some simple questions:

(i) In what ways, if any, do you need to change your behaviours? Are you adapting to the tutors' needs for structure, direction and a sense of purpose?

(ii) In what ways, if any, should the structure of pastoral meetings be improved? Do you need more tutor activity, small group work, a more vigorous commencement, and positive ending?

(iii) Is the timing productive? Long enough, but not over-demanding on time? Can people safely assume that the stated time of finishing will be the actual time?

4.2 Lay out your improvements below in two lists graduated as shown.

(i) *Importance for improvement of pastoral meetings*. (Most important at top, least important at bottom.)

(ii) *Difficulty in implementing*. (Easiest at top, most difficult at bottom.)

4.3 Now examine the differences between the two lists. You may have to compromise between the two aspects, but that is part of management.

Leadership and management skills

The relevant background has been covered in earlier sections and appropriate activities suggested. The remarks here prepare year or house heads for further exercises. There is no fixed style of leadership: we ask what is appropriate for a particular situation. Whatever style is selected, a model of competence has to be given to tutors. A pastoral head must build the confidence of tutors, but that means they must be people in whom the tutors can have confidence. A balanced approach is necessary: knowing when to push and be task-focused, realising when to relax and be relationship-orientated. Leadership means therefore the capacity for self-evaluation and standpoint-taking. It means asking how the tutors see the situation and what motives they attribute to the leader. Gradually one learns what can be tackled in a direct way, and where it would be more profitable to wait or deal indirectly with the matter. The mingled effects of anxiety and omnipotence have to be recognised. Do you feel it all depends on you? Does the desire for results or the urge to prove your effectiveness cause you to ignore or suppress the contributions of others? Leadership depends partly on making goals and objectives clear, but how do you do this? Do you treat objectives as immutable once set, or as open to negotiation?

The first introductory activity touches on time-management, forward planning and delegation. Management of time is the most urgent issue pastoral heads need to tackle. The claim of lack of time is not dishonest yet we may be perpetuating the problem by not sorting out our priorities. The old 20/80 rule breaks into the impasse. What are the 20% of current problems on which we should spend 80% of our time? We become anxious and react to the anxiety by procrastination. It is easy to become immersed in frenetic activity where we drown in a flood of minor activities. Things can be done at the wrong level: this is evasion of responsibility and misuse of time.

Introductory activity on management skills for pastoral heads

1 The intent of the activity

1.1 To begin a preliminary examination of your management of time.

1.2 To allow you to discuss your style of management and leadership, and begin to evaluate your strengths and weaknesses as a manager.
1.3 To examine the need for planning ahead and other skills of organisation.

2 The management of time

2.1 Work in groups of four.
2.2 Begin by identifying sources of waste of time, eg over-long or unproductive pastoral meetings. Ask if the content and interaction of pastoral meetings focus on significant issues and deepen knowledge and skills, or are they concerned with super-ficialities that could be dealt with without the meeting? What causes such meetings to last longer than seems necessary? Put your list on a large sheet of paper; indicate what you consider to be the items that should be given immediate con-sideration. Discuss the implications with another group of four.
2.3 Time is inelastic, therefore it is important to look at our own utilisation of time. Many heads of year or house come into school very early, but to what use do they put this time? It could be used as a block of undisturbed time for planning or developing training activities. Are free periods frittered away or do we plan their use in advance? Prepare an outline of your average working day. Look for periods where, with relatively little effort, you could reorganise yourself, using time more effectively, increasing your sense of competence.
      Discuss with a different group the results of your examination.
2.4 Are you doing things at the wrong level? For example, as a head of year or house you may be doing work which should be done by the form tutor, eg checking registers in detail or admonishing pupils about trivialities. If you shed this misuse of

middle management time what would you do
instead? Many poorly trained pastoral heads seem
to use 'lack of time' – due to too many low-level
and inappropriate tasks – as an excuse to avoid
their middle management responsibilities of leadership and training. Discuss this with another member
of your group of four. After ten minutes, both join up
with another pair with whom you have not
previously worked to continue the discussion.

2.5   Can you think of other ways of creating time? eg
more delegation to form tutors; use of the summer
term after the fifth year have left; more self-
managed learning in the fourth and fifth years;
getting rid of redundant duties, which although
unnecessary, have acquired a sense of 'rightness';
or simple co-operation between pastoral heads
where one does duties setting another free to train
or lead on a *quid pro quo* basis. In different groups
of four explore the possibilities, charting them with
appropriate detail on your large sheets of paper.

3 Your style of leadership and management

3.1 The use of time is closely associated with style of
management and leadership. Leadership involves
negotiation and adaptation. There is no global style
of leadership, but one which fits a particular
situation. The efficient head of year or house asks:
   (i) What do I need from my tutors? Can I specify
       this clearly and precisely?
Work out *in pairs* what is required from tutors by
undertaking:
   ● *A job analysis*: this says *what* has to be done;
   ● *A skills analysis*: this says *how* it will be done
     (eg skills of small group work, decision-making
     and problem-solving approaches.)
   (ii) Look at how your leadership style must adapt
       to the current attitudes and level of skills of
       tutors, eg if attitudes veer towards the negative

and skills are low, then clearer structure, firmer support and more initiation of activity by the leader is necessary. This is expressed positively and energetically. Other groups may need a more relaxed and relationship orientated approach.

Remember the effective style can differ with different year or house groups within the school.

Work out the style that you think will be most productive with your tutors. Then in groups of four justify your conclusions, referring to the evidence that supports them.

3.2 Rigidity of style, *viz* an almost automatic reliance on relationships or focusing solely on the tasks, produces friction or dismissal of the pastoral head as ineffective.

In groups of four work out the possible reasons for this self-defeating rigidity.

4 Other aspects of management

4.1 Planning ahead, anticipating difficulties, and being prepared well in advance, are obviously important. It may not be quite so palpable that the ability to analyse important relationships in depth is crucial for planning and management. What is detected can then be incorporated into one's strategies.

Take the following examples and assess the relationships as closely as possible. Work in groups of four and chart your analyses on large sheets of paper.

- a particular year considered from the pastoral viewpoint of other years; eg year two where many difficulties first manifest themselves;
- the pastoral subsystem *or* your year or house to certain academic departments;
- the pastoral system to parents.

4.2 We can distinguish between forward planning and

forward strategic planning. Forward planning is based on the known; forward strategic planning is the response to what is unknown – what may happen. It is concerned with the anticipation of discontinuities from the past and other changes which are largely unpredictable. We can search for possibilities, detect trends, threats, opportunities and crises. By focusing on contingencies we can develop potential ways of dealing with the situations if they arise. This means we can deal with them competently rather than being 'caught on the hop'. We therefore avoid becoming the victims of circumstances. Forward strategic planning is neither a luxury nor a waste of time: for as we think ahead we see many possibilities; current issues and paths to goals are illuminated; whilst middle management acquires a sense of potency.

In groups of four assess:
  (i)   the nature and efficiency of current planning in the pastoral team;
 (ii)   ways of improving it;
(iii)   the importance of *forward strategic planning*, and the ways in which the skills associated with it can be acquired – you will, of course, have to define the skills.

Prepare a brief presentation of 20 minutes duration on (i) to (iii) and give it to another group of four.

---

5 A few factors touching on important aspects of organisation:

5.1 Delegation, ie the entrusting of authority and power to others.
  (i)   Briefly examine in groups of six the use of delegation in your school. Do you consider there is effective use, under-use or misuse of delegation in the school? Justify your opinions.
 (ii)   Work out what you consider to be the criteria for the practice of delegation.

(iii) What delegation occurs in the team of pastoral heads? Evaluate it. Make recommendations for change if you feel it would be helpful. If you would endorse the existing state of affairs do so. Whatever position you take, please support it by reasoned argument.

5.2 Planning is concerned with knitting together the elements of pastoral activity.

(i) Alertness to, and anticipation of, snags and unwanted outcomes. In pairs list some of these things, eg the same topics being covered in tutor periods and in subjects without any consultation. Share ideas in groups of six.

(ii) Precise details of the arrangements for modifying the pastoral programme after evaluation, training tutors or developing materials that meet the needs of the school.

In groups of four select *one* point and discuss in as much depth as possible. (You are not restricted to the examples given.)

(iii) The arrangements for raising the level of performances of form tutors and heads of year or house. In groups of six look closely at what is needed and make detailed and realistic recommendations. Your focus should be on what can be done by the staff within the school.

Pastoral heads: leadership skills – a developmental exercise

1 The intent of the exercise

1.1 To stress the adaptive and situational nature of middle management pastoral leadership.

1.2 To help pastoral heads discuss the fundamental elements of leadership.

1.3 To provide some experience of assessing the readiness of their tutors for further development.

2 Four basic elements

2.1 The work of Hersey and Blanchard (1977) on situational leadership and Howard *et al* (1987) on adaptive counselling and therapy asks how much directive and how much supportive behaviour will be needed in particular leadership situations. For this exercise we need to distinguish between *personal preferences* of the leader and the *needs of the group of tutors*, accepting that some individual variations will exist.

2.2 Assess first your personal preferences for the four styles set out below. Please be as honest as possible: some may appear more desirable than others.

1 *Telling* provides high direction and low support. It may be necessary when tutors are unwilling, lack knowledge and skills and have little confidence.

2 *Teaching* gives both high direction and support, and is claimed to be useful when people are unable and unwilling.

3 *Supporting* is marked by low direction and high support. It is indicated when group members are able and willing, but have little confidence.

4 *Delegating* is marked by low direction *and* low support. It can be productive when group members are skilled, willing and confident.

2.3 *Discuss*:

1 The significance of any preference for one style you possess. Is it likely to be productive with your tutors?

2 If you use more than one style – this may include ones not mentioned above – what are your criteria for employing them in particular situations?

3 Which style is likely to be very unproductive with your tutors? Why? Grade the four styles in what you believe will be their productivity with your tutors. (1 is high – 4 is low.) Explain your reasons.

3 Assessing tutor readiness for developing pastoral work

3.1 A first step is to describe the strengths and weaknesses of your tutors' current performance.

3.2 This is necessary but not sufficient. Make a list of the *attitudes* and *behaviours* you would assess in considering your tutors' readiness to move from the *status quo*. Because they are coping at one level of pastoral work, there is no guarantee they can cope with more advanced demands, or want to.

ATTITUDES	BEHAVIOURS
1 *Resistant to development or will create blocks:*	3 *Resistant to development or will create blocks:*
2 *Support change and development:*	4 *Support change and development:*

Another simple activity is to explore tutors' convictions about 'things/approaches that work' and 'things/approaches' that do not work.

3.3 Summarise the readiness of your tutors for further development in pastoral work.

4 Specifying change/development

4.1 Set out below as precisely as possible the developments you would like to stimulate. (Use behavioural terms as much as possible, eg 'praise pupils for effort' rather than 'have positive attitudes'.)

5 Selecting a leadership style

5.1 Which of the four styles (or any other you think relevant) would you *use to launch the developments* with your group of tutors? Explain the reasons for your choice as fully as possible.

The skills of planning ahead and forward strategic planning
[This activity requires a considerable amount of time. It could make the basis for an INSET day for year or house heads.]

1 The intent of this activity sheet

1.1 To raise key issues concerned with development for discussion by the pastoral team.
1.2 To provide an outline model for development and response to change which can be adapted by pastoral heads.
1.3 To help participants think constructively and practically about managing resistance to development and having strategies – note the plural – for implementing the new approaches.

2 STEP ONE: Developing and sharpening a forward-looking orientation

2.1 *Questions for discussion*
(i) What will make the future different from the past? Is it possible that teachers will have to accept a greater rate of change, hopefully in a climate of support rather than one of devaluation?
(ii) What changes will developments such as the National Curriculum make? How might this influence the ability of the pastoral system to achieve its objectives or modify those objectives? Teachers cannot assume that the future will automatically be better than the past.

2.2 Rudduck (1986) argues that effective change depends on building a shared understanding of the proposed developments among the members of 'the working group'. Without this, developments will fail. Ansoff (1984) points out that organisations under stress move back to an earlier way of behaving as soon as possible. Rudduck mentions an inevitable distortion in communication which results in the new being turned into some version of the old: change is apparent rather than real.

Discuss the practical implications of this for your developmental role. What initiatives are likely to provoke such responses? What conditions facilitate or inhibit them? *List* the key elements you believe would determine a successful response to your planning and intended developments.

2.3 Planning is basically a problem-solving process in which you are actively:
   (i) Specifying your changes to concrete terms.
   (ii) Detecting, through active searching, oppor-tunities and problems.
   (iii) Working out which problems require early or forceful attention.
   (iv) Assessing which opportunities offer maximum rewards for investment of effort.
   (v) Looking for the most effective ways of making the first steps, anticipating any difficulties, and making arrangements for early feedback.

2.4 *Activity*:
   As a preliminary planning step, quickly work through the steps in 2.3 making notes below on their significance for you.

3 STEP TWO: Diagnosis as a planning skill

3.1 Planning ahead requires problem solving firmly rooted in diagnosis. Strategies for development use means–ends thinking and the ability to work out the sequence of steps that have to be taken. Planning also involves anticipation (this sounds tautological) but it means gathering resources, creating a climate for acceptance of proposals, and having realistic ideas about the nature of resistances and ways of overcoming them.

Diagnosis is your first step:

(i) Where does the power lie? Have shifts in power recently occurred as a result of amalgamation, recent appointments, the development of *intra*-staff conflict or management policies? Are parents or governors included in your considerations?

(ii) Hamblin draws attention to the Mannheimian view of truth – the truth of pastoral care and its development partially depends on your position in a social structure. The disjunctions between the viewpoints of senior management and form tutors could make attempts at development abortive unless they are taken into account. Quickly sketch out the salient elements of the views of the following *as a group* about pastoral care:

- senior management;
- heads of academic departments;
- pastoral heads;
- class teachers;
- pupils.

What does this mean for your planning?

(iii) What conflicts about priorities exist in the school? Will they impinge on your plans? How? Make a brief statement below.

3.2 The planner wants to emphasise continuity *where possible* so that the security of those involved in the change is not threatened unnecessarily. The effective planner asks, 'What is there I can build on?' *More of the good that exists* is a sound foundation for change. The familiar and successful should be used without distorting or denying the changes. *List* what could be used as a foundation below.

    Such approaches are concerned with gaining

credibility for you as a planner and your plans. They also reduce the 'perceived gap' between the old and the new.

3.3 Diagnosis includes asking what has become obsolescent – it sounds mechanical, but is vital. GCSE has left some teachers in difficulties because learning – and the complex psychological issues of relating it to personality – has assumed importance. Not only do we need to create an adaptive learning environment, we have also to wrestle with the deeper implications of the changes in the model of the effective learner. This leads to consideration of the 'mentality gap' (Ansoff's phrase) between current knowledge and attitude of colleagues and the demands of change. (Sadly, previous strengths could become liabilities.)

3.4 Ask how the current *value climate* of the school relates to your plans. What is seen as important by the majority of staff? Is there consensus, overt or implicit, on certain value-laden issues, eg punishment, achievement or relationships between pupils and teachers? Are you liable to be labelled a 'boat-rocker' etc? How important is this?

3.5 You should now have a fair idea of the supports available, and the opposition you face.

---

4 STEP THREE: Structuring your plans

4.1 State your plans as succinctly and clearly as possible below. Be concrete, describing the behaviours and skills you wish colleagues to acquire. Include a brief justification for your plans.

4.2 Think in terms of 'piecemeal' objectives (Davies, 1976), ie breaking the global change down into 'pieces' or short units. It is a step-by-step approach in which objectives are sharpened within the total plan. It allows constructive negotiation with those involved, and adaptation to anticipated consequences.

Break your plan down into a number of units.

4.3 *A critical point*: *Planning and implementation go together*. Pastoral heads and others involved should be actively planning and refining the next step or stage as the current one is implemented. Feedback from the implementation should be sought and used to adapt the planning to the difficulties and positive factors that are emerging. *The reasons for this include the likelihood that*:

(i) Attitudes are more likely to change when people do something; attitude change follows behaviour, and does not always have to precede behaviour.

(ii) Resistance is reduced if colleagues feel they are not being pushed into global change.

(iii) There are opportunities for decisions and involvement at the beginning of each unit.

Outline your reactions to this approach to management and planning.

5 Strategic forward planning

5.1 Ansoff (1984) writing about change in industry and commerce, comments on the growth of discontinuities and unpredictable change. This also applies to schools, and means that *past experience is no longer a reliable guide to the future*.

Strategic forward planning requires disciplined imagination in assessing possibilities. Existing trends are used as indicators of what the future *might* hold, but it is not assumed that they allow accurate predictions. The style of thought is that of Piaget's Formal Operations where the thinker works on an 'if this . . . then this' basis using hypothetical-deductive thinking which suggests possible relationships before they are present in reality.

Senior and middle management will have to adopt this style of thinking as part of their planning ahead in what Ansoff calls a 'turbulent environment'. Put simply, we have to go beyond current situations and have answers for possibilities so that we do not flounder or passively react. This surely will give us a sense of competence and mastery.

5.2 Look at current trends in the curriculum. Speculate what impact they might have on the structure and content of pastoral activity.

5.3 How is the teacher's role likely to change in the next 10–15 years? Anticipate the impact of this on pastoral work.

5.4 We have seen welcome links between industry and schools. What else might happen which would change the form and function of schools, and consequently that of pastoral activity?

The message:
Dynamic pastoral care needs a lively management team who think deeply about issues and who refuse to be intimidated by pettifogging activity whatever its source.

Linking the pastoral and curricular

Linking the pastoral and curricular
This topic was discussed in reasonable depth in the preceding chapter. Pastoral heads will find the exercise stimulating. The standpoint-taking exercise (4) has proved extremely illuminating, revealing basic assumptions about colleagues' reactions.

Integrating pastoral work with curriculum developments

1 The intent of this exercise

1.1 To encourage pastoral heads to think seriously of ways in which the pastoral and curricular should be linked.

1.2 To identify areas of interaction and co-operation between pastoral and academic middle management.

1.3 To understand the processes operating within the school which constrain pupils' learning and performance, thereby reducing the teachers' rewards for their hard work.

1.4 To consider possibilities for joint research with academic heads on pupils' learning, and work out subsequent developments in tutor group activities.

2 Questions for exploration

2.1 What changes in teaching and learning have occurred which could be followed up in tutor work with benefit to all?

You probably listed target setting, self-assessment and decision making but what of other skills such as co-operation? The traditional classroom was sometimes the place where a pupil could perform successfully with minimal interaction with others. Now pupils need to have the skills of positive interaction in groups as part of their repertoire of learning skills.

(i) List the skills you would develop for each year group, ie years one to six. (You may focus on one year, if this is helpful.)

(ii) State how you would foster the skills in tutor work. Look carefully at this, and even more closely at the ways you would build links between the tutor periods and the classroom.

2.2 What general views of learning are held by:

(i) pupils;

(ii) teachers?

Do they match? If there is a mismatch, what is the significance of this? How will you check that your impressions of pupils' viewpoints are accurate? On what evidence are they based? Is this a key area for action research?

2.3 It may be productive to consider the approach to two particularly crucial years in more depth.

(i) *The second year* where a sizeable proportion of pupils are beginning to dissociate from the values and objectives of the school. They doubt their ability, or have little desire, to meet the demands school is making on them. They are absent in the spirit, although still present in the flesh.

(ii) *Year four* where pupils are beginning to make a dichotomy between life in school and their social life – to the detriment of their performance at school. They need to develop self- and time-management skills. Planning and target-setting skills, coupled with realistic self-evaluation, are essential for coping with the challenge of GCSE.

3 Negotiation

3.1 Integrating pastoral and curricular concerns is obviously based in negotiation with heads of academic departments. It may be illuminating and helpful to begin with departments which in ethos and content have clear links with pastoral activity. Work out what is likely to be:
(i) the *content* of the negotiation;
(ii) the *desired and probable* outcomes.
3.2 Now comment on the way you would negotiate with the other subject departments. Beware any tendency to pre-categorisation. Pastoral heads do not always read situations accurately, eg stereotypes about 'resistance' emanating from 'scientists' impede development. There are as many differences among 'scientists' as there are among other subject groups. It may be important to explain clearly your purposes and abandon defensiveness.

4 A standpoint-taking exercise

4.1 Plan a meeting of third, fourth and fifth year heads who are working with the heads of mathematics, geography, English, CDT and home economics exploring ways of linking the pastoral and the classroom activities of pupils.

(i) Imagine this is the fourth meeting. Outline what has gone before.

(ii) Give the agenda for the meeting.

(iii) Move to the end of this, the fourth meeting, and say what you think might have been accomplished, and what obstacles or difficulties still have to be overcome.

Make notes on these points.

4.2 Now discuss, and note, what this says about your perceptions, ideas and predictions about the linkage of the pastoral and curricular in the later years of the secondary school. Critical appraisal is useful – it need not be negative.

---

5 Issues for discussion at middle-management level initially

5.1 What is it that erodes the enthusiasm and apparent capacity for taking responsibility for their learning that pupils show in the primary school? Is it merely developmental factors associated with adolescence or peer group influences?

5.2 In linking the pastoral and curricular we may over-stress transfer from the tutor period to the classroom. Should it not be a two-way process? Should we not undertake classroom research within the school which tutors would follow up in tutor periods?

5.3 We have the impetus of active learning which is welcome but:

(i) How do we prevent pupils retreating to their earlier passive position?

(ii) Can we prevent active learning from becoming an empty ritual, ie losing its purpose and motivating power?

5.4 Are we taking the deeper issues of learning seriously enough? Pupils see school as having a serious purpose, but does this extend to pastoral activity? If pastoral work does not challenge them by exploring learning in depth and purposefully reflecting on classroom experience it deserves to be dismissed as trivial. If the pastoral programme appears unaware of the world of work and does not play a part in careers education and stimulating initiative what has it to offer the older adolescent? Effective middle management must come to terms with these realities.

4 Leading a team of tutors

Leading as team-building

Examples of activities will be found in Chapter Two and in Hamblin (1984). Those pastoral heads who have worked through with their colleagues the exercises in Chapter Three should be clearer about their leadership roles and the nature of pastoral work, and may have personal theories of development and change. They will have seen that we may over-concentrate on teacher/adolescent relationships at the cost of adult/adult relationships. Yet the former may be improved by greater consideration of the latter. The need for knowledge and skill in giving effective support and leadership to tutors should also be evident.

In this chapter we shall briefly look at building a team in which tutors have a sense of responsibility. Consideration will then be given to certain aspects of learning about learning. Staff stress will be dealt with in practical ways, as in coping with difficult behaviours in the classroom and the skills of defusing situations.

What may be called for is a major reorientation in the way pastoral heads work with their tutors. Bradford and Cohen (1984) put forward fundamental assumptions that pastoral heads can usefully employ in leading their tutor teams. First, they emphasise that most people can change, calling attention to the *self-fulfilling consequences of the belief that people cannot, or will not, change*. Second, and vital, is their insistence that *leadership should be about creating the conditions which increase the likelihood of success for team members*. This means building skills: the power of the leader is therefore enabling rather than restrictive.

A team sharing responsibility, actively engaging in problem solving, is the ideal towards which we strive. The first step is to make the important concept of ownership a reality in tutor work. Unless tutors are involved in developing and appraising activities, they retreat to the belief that pastoral work is for 'the expert'. Next, pastoral heads need to share the problems with which they are grappling, developing involved engagement in tackling them. What has to be dealt with first can only be decided within a particular school and tutor team: no recipes are available. The above does not imply evasion. The problems of limited conceptions of pastoral work as 'shoulders to cry on', 'sorting them out', abortive punishment or generally as something that has no links with the teachers' mainstream task have to be faced. Pastoral heads will seek to understand such positions but this does not mean endorsing them. Courage is needed as false conceptions are studied, and then modified.

Tutors should be encouraged to incorporate their own activities into the pastoral programme, gaining a sense of ownership and independence. This is a *gradual* process. It is productive because a tutor operating at a professional level knows what will be relevant to his or her tutor group; has ideas about appropriate forms of activity and presentation of the topic that call out a positive response from the form; and the sequence of topics that will suit the group. Certain pastoral heads produce a programme, expect rigid adherence to it, and are then puzzled by lack of enthusiasm. It is more productive to give specimen activities, encourage critical appraisal of them, and allow tutors to build their own. They then explain the activities to fellow tutors, justifying them, and seeking ideas for their extension.

Involvement is enhanced if pastoral heads and their teams undertake some simple research into pupils' felt needs. Pupils' conceptions of their needs are part, although I stress, only part, of the data used to construct a pastoral programme suited to a particular group. There should be a determined, continuous enquiry into the ways in which pupils can become participants in their own guidance: partners with tutors and pastoral heads rather than mere recipients. We begin by letting them construct their own decision-making and problem-solving activities for use in their own, and other, forms. Year or house heads or tutors may therefore have to teach the skills of constructing activities to pupils, enhancing co-operation by a uniquely pastoral version of active learning.

Joint work on identification of problems which bedevil pupils provides a 'frame' within which tutors apprehend the developmental purposes of pastoral work. Problems of loss of interest after the third year, growth of identity through opposition, and pupils' suspicions that autonomy is eroded by pastoral activity are best overcome by this partnership perspective.

Heads of year or house will profit from simulating their proposed training sessions. One of them presents the intended session, whilst the others act as tutors. They then appraise its likely effectiveness. The framework presented below has been effective in training sessions.

Building a training programme for tutors

1 Objectives

1.1 To allow course members to examine the possibilities of developing tutor training within the school.
1.2 To develop an outline programme of training.
1.3 In co-operation with others, participants will produce one training session in detail.

2 Activity one: Preliminary discussion work in groups of four

2.1 What resources exist within your school other than the team of pastoral heads? (Some teachers have particular skills at graphics, the production of video-tapes or the construction of problem-solving activities. Their involvement will widen the content of the training programme helpfully.)
2.2 How will you deal with the following?
   (i) The misconceptions of some teachers about the nature of pastoral work eg 'an inferior welfare system'.
   (ii) Anxieties about control and discipline.
   (iii) The feeling that it is yet another demand with which they cannot cope.
   (iv) The belief that tutor group activity has little connection with learning and the mainstream tasks of the school.
2.3 How would you begin your first attempts at training a group of tutors:
   (i) begin with the enthusiastic;
   (ii) consult with the group about what they would find useful;

(iii) use an INSET day for the whole school or begin in a less ostentatious way?

2.4 Training implies leadership that adapts to the current state of affairs: in some schools more structure and guidance will be needed than in others. What works in one school will not work in another. Before approaching the construction of your package it may be useful to assess:

  (i) The content and rigidity of existing norms about the nature and purpose of pastoral activity.

  (ii) Do these norms stem from the system? For example, if there is not a whole-school policy on positive discipline and striving for ideals, then pastoral work can become swamped by abortive punishments. Long-standing tensions and dissatisfactions may lie behind habitual opposition to change.

  (iii) Ask how you will work with the opinion leaders who will influence the reactions of others.

(Obviously, time will not allow full discussion of these issues, but ideas can be generated for later use.)

3 Activity two: Planning an outline training package of six to eight sessions of one hour's duration

3.1 *Work in groups of four.*

3.2 State clearly the objectives of the *total* package and also each training session.

3.3 Ensure that you will be able to meet the objections of those who doubt the usefulness of pastoral work. Anticipation and ways of coping will be facilitated by considering the following:

  (i) Discuss with a partner how you would cope with the responses set out below:

'I'm paid to teach!'

'I'm not here to molly-coddle them.'

'We are doing it already.'
'Are you saying pastoral care will solve all our discipline problems?'

(ii) Strategies should avoid aggressiveness. Where possible take the wind out of their sails by agreeing as the first step in helping them look at their position eg Statement (i) would lead into a discussion of good teaching and creating a productive climate for learning. Statement (ii) brings one to look at giving pupils the skills of coping. Statement (iii) would be dealt with by getting them to explore what they are doing, you gradually make suggestions for extension. Statement (iv) could be reflected back and they should be asked if they believe that anything could achieve this. Reality is then brought in. An appeal to common sense can be made with humour, eg, 'I'm sure you don't really believe I'm so foolish . . .'

(iii) Now make a list of remarks that could dis-organise you. In small groups share ideas about constructive replies or responses which divest the remarks of their sting.

3.4 Once you have decided on the topics they have to be placed in sequence. Please spell out the justifications for the sequence you select. Does it involve increasing complexity and depth or build logically on what has gone before?

3.5 Training is a form of learning: this means a dialogue between content and process. How will tutors acquire the skills and attitudes and apply the knowledge? The history of previous training or innovation is relevant; eg some teachers have felt threatened by insensitive use of role play.

(i) The balance between trainer input and tutor activity is a critical element: training is about active learning!

(ii) Another prime consideration is the way in which your training programme involves trainees in developing their own materials and ideas – the sense of *ownership* of pastoral activity is vital.

3.6 Ask how the activities and training will help the teacher get greater satisfaction from a taxing and demanding job.

---

4 Activity three: Developing a training session

4.1 State as clearly as possible the objectives of the session. For example:
- What skills do you want participants to acquire?
- What knowledge do you want them to acquire?
- Do you wish them to reach a decision or decisions?
- Are they required to revise their opinions?
- Should they evaluate specific things, eg the needs of a particular group or the effectiveness of certain aspects of pastoral care?

(These points merely illustrate some of the possibilities.)

4.2 Detail
- (i) The length of the training session.
- (ii) Your intended balance between trainer input and trainee activity. (Is it roughly equal, or two thirds trainee activity to one third trainer input?) Justify the balance by referring to the needs of the group, their readiness for change and/or other relevant factors.
- (iii) The major activities you will include, eg decisions based on a case study, problem solving, the construction of materials or role play. Be as specific as possible about the reasons for choosing them.
- (iv) The materials needed by trainers and trainees. (Good, well planned sessions have foundered because materials of a simple kind have not been available.)

4.3 *Outline of the session*:
Give your plans for the session in sufficient detail for other trainers to be able to use it. Pay special attention to:

(i) The opening activity. Does it attract attention of a positive kind? Does it have an authentic quality about it? Is it motivating?

(ii) The sequence: a good training session is one where each activity clearly relates to the preceding and succeeding one.

(iii) The final activity which should leave a feeling of success or positive challenge in participants' minds. Does it encourage their involvement in planning later sessions?

(iv) The materials and activities needed for each sub-phase or activity and the time allocated to it.

The opening phase:
Describe it as fully as possible. This often determines the success of the session.

4.4 *Other activities or sub-stages*:
Briefly indicate how they lead on to the next one or develop what has gone before. Check your timings carefully. Describe each activity briefly. Underline anything the trainers should keep in mind.

Two simple approaches to evaluation are now given. The first looks at the individual(s) giving the training session, and then moves to the structure and content. The second is based on standpoint-taking.

1 Individual assessments

1.1 What seemed to be your strengths and weaknesses in the training session? When you have listed them, get a fellow pastoral head to give his comments on your self-evaluation.

1.2 How could you build on the strengths?

1.3 Work out a plan for dealing with your weaknesses. use a 'one step at a time' approach. Begin with the areas in which you feel you are most likely to succeed.

1.4 What supports could you draw on?

2 The simulated session

2.1 How well was it introduced? Did I:
- gain participants' attention;
- keep the pace going in a way which made people feel I had a sense of purpose and there was something worthwhile to achieve;
- allow them to become active as quickly as possible;
- use visual aids to reinforce or supplement what I said?

(Please add any other points.)

2.2 Was the balance of trainer input and tutor activity productive for this group?

2.3 If more than one person was involved in the training was the balance, sequence and 'mix' of person-alities, manner and voices the most productive that could have been achieved? Did we pay sufficient attention to using the individual's strengths?

2.4 Did the closing activity reinforce the sense of achievement of participants? What impression would be left in their minds of:
- pastoral activity;
- the role of the tutor;
- the trainer(s)?

2.5 Did the participants have the opportunity to con-tribute ideas? Did they feel their suggestions were being used and respected?

2.6 How would you elicit feedback from them after the session?

A standpoint-taking approach

1 Write a report on your training session as if:
   (i) you were a tutor who appreciates the impor-tance of pastoral work.
   (ii) you were a tutor who is unconvinced, perhaps negative, about the value of pastoral activity.

Try to write from the standpoint of tutors who form part of your team and not merely give a positive or negative assessment. See it through their eyes, although you have to accept that your interpretation of their viewpoint cannot be totally accurate.

(iii) With a colleague, examine the implications of the contrasting viewpoints for your future planning and training.

2 Next, carefully examine the congruencies and discrepancies between your objectives and what you did in the simulation. The latter is 'ideas in action'. How did it fit the ideas to which you subscribe? Try to explain any inconsistencies.

Let me stress the importance of preliminary simulations with the group of year and house heads. They actually foster team work and build on individuals' confidence. Tutors need a model of competence from the year or house head with which to compare themselves.

Pastoral leadership for learning about learning

The self as a learner is the major element in the output of the secondary school. Students take it into their first job, further and higher education, yet this essential product of school experience is rarely monitored in depth. We are aware of the changing character of learning tasks, but do we work to change the students' perceptions of themselves as learners and of learning? Marland *et al* (1981) grasp the essential when they say we need not only learning and problem solving in the classroom context, but the didactic, ie learners clarifying principles and verbalising skills. The basic task is, as Hamblin (1981) argues, that of taking a developmental approach in which students develop an appropriate style of learning and a cognitive style rooted in personality. Extroverts will therefore have a different learning style from that of introverts; those marked by high susceptibility to anxiety may need to structure their learning more sharply than the less anxious: they need to boost their sense of control and be more positive in their predictions; doubt incapacitates them. Teachers' recipes are suspect: probably ineffective; possibly harmful. Tutor periods must offer opportunities to reflect on learning, helping students identify, verbalise and justify the strategies they believe will suit them in tackling a specific learning task. In co-operation with subject teachers, tutors prepare pupils for experimenting with their application in the classroom. Linking the pastoral and curricular is then a reality. Passive knowledge is inadequate; it has to be translated into action. Recently, I have become severely diabetic. I know what my diet should be; but do I apply that knowledge? Pastoral heads also need to help tutors consider how they will use in their classrooms what they initiate in tutor periods. This increases the rewards they get for investing energy in pastoral work.

Value issues have to be tackled energetically in pastoral leadership. Teachers and pupils alike need to clarify their values after critical examination. A proper recognition that education involves preparation for a post-industrial world does not mean that learning in school is to be valued solely as preparation for the future. Dewey long ago commented on the loss of moral power inherent in this viewpoint. Such a view gives pupils no defence against the concept of economic man who is a totally rational being engaged in maximising his satisfactions according to materialistic criteria. Does altruism have any part to play? This unacknowledged model of man has a pervasive effect on learning and the perceptions of subjects which we ignore. Pupils also have false perceptions of the nature and significance of subjects, and of those who are good at them.

Goodman's (1984) work merits earnest consideration by all concerned with learning. He points out that we have to accommodate conflicting 'truths' without sacrificing the difference between truth and falsity. Wall (1948) shows that adolescent development includes the philosophical self. I see this world view as a fundamental element in adolescent learning which filters and allocates meaning to experience, and eventually dominates the individual's interpretation of events. Goodman talks in a broader sense of 'world making', but I also see adolescent learning as a process of individual world making which should be discussed in pastoral guidance.

Goodman shows the urgent need to discard the false oppositions we make between the sciences and arts. It is thoughtless to behave as if science strives for truth and the arts strive for beauty. Both use evidence in a disciplined way; both are subjective; fostering of originality is needed in both. Pastoral heads and tutors would benefit from examining Goodman's contention that art and science are inextricable; emotion and cognition interdependent. In an age where spirit is devalued and power exalted, learning about learning could well be based on his view that feeling without understanding is blind; understanding without feeling empty. There is hope now that GCSE syllabi present a wider view – including, for example, recognition of the importance of empathy – that the 'venerable but untenable dichotomies' between the cognitive and emotive are being challenged, maybe discarded.

Pupils therefore need to discard easy dichotomies of 'true or false' for 'probably true', 'probably false', 'true', 'false' or 'insufficient data'. This, of course, is not a statement about the nature of truth, but indicates the level of confidence one can have in the inferences made. Creativity should be prime. Herbert Read (1958) stressed the function of art in developing structure 'where none existed or providing an alternative to what exists.' It 'is the ability to see relationships where none were seen, the capacity to discard assumptions temporarily, and view problems from a different standpoint.' (Quotations from Hamblin, 1983). All this is orientated towards achievement, taking the viewpoint of Whitehead (1959) who argued that a major aim of education is to produce people who not only *know* something well but are capable of *doing* something well.

GCSE attempts this by demanding greater initiative from pupils, the skills of decision making in tackling assignments, and small group co-operation. Realism demands recognition of the ways in which pupils subvert these aims, such as through dependency behaviours to which the insecure or unconvinced teacher responds by telling them exactly what to do, abandoning the objectives. Pastoral periods must foster analysis of the broad processes of learning as well as examining personal reactions to learning tasks. Far too many pupils reach the fourth and fifth forms seeing learning as amorphous: either something they can or cannot do. They do not see it as something they can control and own; an activity susceptible to analysis and planned rational action. The exercise below has been used on many occasions to open up discussion and plan an initial module on learning about learning.

Learning about learning

1 Developing a wider orientation

1.1 Discuss the implications of the following statements about learning:
(i) The teacher can no longer simply ask, 'What should students know about my subject?' but should ask, 'How can I through my subject prepare them for a rapidly-changing world?' (Adapted from *IFAPLAN*, Brussels.)
(ii) Marland *et al* (1981) in *Informational Skills in the Secondary School* argue that we need not only learning in context but discussion of the principles and methods of learning by pupils creating awareness of their learning style.
(iii) The real problems may not lie in techniques but in motivation, eg 'I mean to get started on my revision when I go in, but somehow I can't.'

2 Questions about achievement

2.1 QUESTION: (i) What ideas about the nature of success should we foster in a rapidly-changing society?
(ii) How can the pastoral team consistently and effectively promote the realistic desire to achieve and encourage standards of excellence?

2.2 SHARE: Ideas about negotiating and developing a long-term programme of guidance which looks at skills, attitudes and motivation. The diagram below may help.

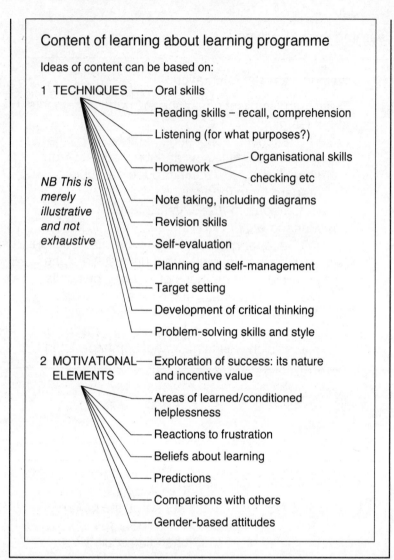

Content of learning about learning programme

Ideas of content can be based on:

1 TECHNIQUES —— Oral skills

Reading skills – recall, comprehension

Listening (for what purposes?)

Homework
- Organisational skills
- checking etc

Note taking, including diagrams

Revision skills

Self-evaluation

Planning and self-management

Target setting

Development of critical thinking

Problem-solving skills and style

NB This is merely illustrative and not exhaustive

2 MOTIVATIONAL ELEMENTS —— Exploration of success: its nature and incentive value

Areas of learned/conditioned helplessness

Reactions to frustration

Beliefs about learning

Predictions

Comparisons with others

Gender-based attitudes

3 A broader view

3.1 If there are processes which impinge upon pupils and constrain their performance, making their teachers' hard work less effective than it could be, then it seems sensible to deal with them in a systematic way.

3.2 Examples of such things include:
  (i) *Learned helplessness* or unchallenged beliefs that the individual cannot succeed in certain areas. They are supported by such justifications as 'None of my family have ever been good at . . .', 'If I do try I only . . .'.
  (ii) *False beliefs/stereotypes about the nature of certain subjects* and the kind of people who are good at them.
  (iii) *Unquestioned gender-based assumptions* about ability.
  (iv) Inadequate *skills of self-management*.
  (v) *The attribution of responsibility* for success to others, eg when frustration occurs in learning, rather than tackling it rationally, the response is 'The school's no good; they don't teach you properly there; the teachers say they care, but they don't really!'
  (vi) *Self-defeating behaviours*, eg pretending they do not care and opting out when they find real challenge.
  (vii) Unquestioned *reliance upon luck* and chance.
  Construct your own list of factors which inhibit performance.
3.3 Develop suggestions about the ways in which pastoral activity could tackle these things which insidiously undermine the hard work of the teacher. Take as positive an approach as possible. The development of the skills of formative assessment and target-setting by pupils may be especially important.

Learning tasks could be presented in tutor work. Pupils work in small groups assessing the way they could be tackled. Groups then describe their ideas, explaining the reasons for their choice. Doyle (1983) distinguishes between:

1 Memory tasks
2 Routine tasks where a particular formula has to be followed

3 Comprehension or understanding tasks where knowledge has to be applied to new problems, and/or inferential thinking is necessary
4 Opinion tasks – but the evidence which supports the opinion must be clarified.

Discussion and activities can be built around these categories. Creating awareness of them is the first step in changing pupils' perception of learning as psychological regurgitation.

Tutors must assist pupils to take a healthily suspicious glance at their classroom behaviours. From time out of mind pupils have learned ways of satisfying teachers by superficial responses. Staving off trouble in the short run; robbing Peter to pay Paul as a way of dealing with conflicting adult/peer obligations; spotting the socially desirable responses which satisfy the busy teacher; and superficial compliance with demands are typical examples. Pastoral work does not entail a 'trailing clouds of glory' approach to the adolescent – that may be rather damp. Facts have to be faced. Elkind (1970), interpreting and applying the work of Piaget, talks about a strong tendency for the child to see himself as clever and the adult as bumbling and stupid. *Cognitive conceit*, as Elkind forthrightly calls it, leads the adolescent to dismiss the teacher's suggestions as unnecessary or unworkable. A limited conception of task requirements is then taken as the full reality. Themes of outwitting adults frequently emerge in adolescent fantasy and group counselling: have we taken them sufficiently seriously as part of classroom learning?

Doyle (1983) examines pupils' evasion of demands and their vigilant responses to the evaluatory dimensions of classroom life. He provides a fascinating account of pupils' strategies for manipulating teachers and coping with ambiguity and risk in the classroom. Provisional answers are given to elicit feedback from the teacher before selecting a precise answer. When active learning and initiative is required, pressure is put on the teacher to provide structure and give a clear indication of the desired outcome.

Teachers are bombarded with questions and appeals at the point where the lesson switches from 'listen to me' to 'do this'. Appeals are made which, if responded to inappropriately, reduce pupils' exploratory behaviours and initiative. Pupils exploit the fact that if they appear confused or helpless, the teacher is likely to tell them what to do, giving them an 'easy ride'. (It may be worth noting that teachers on courses display such tendencies: staff developers can then be nonplussed.) Doyle, describing similar behaviours, sees them as expressions of pupils' deep-seated beliefs that they have the right to be told what to do. Failure to explore these matters in tutor periods is collusion with underfunctioning. Tutors could undertake classroom observations focused on such behaviours. Reactions to intervention by the teacher are assessed; threats to pupils' self-esteem are identified and measures developed. Realism suggests that pupils cannot easily discard relatively long-held assumptions about the teacher's work and the nature of learning.

McCombs (1988) highlights the importance of Bandura's self-efficacy theory. *Perceived* competence and a personal sense of control are postulated as essential for motivation. Rotter *et al* (1972) and Phares (1976) stress the consequences of perceptions of control as either external or internal; Covington and Beery (1976) examine the impact of self-esteem, or its lack, on learning. There is considerable evidence that positive perceptions of individual responsibility are crucial for continued striving for success. There is a tension between the global assertions of such research and reported classroom observation such as that of Doyle. It becomes imperative that pastoral leaders encourage focused observation by tutors and, with academic heads, assess the meaning of pupils' classroom behaviours.

The gist of recent work is less problematic: pupils should be encouraged to think about the ways they tackle learning tasks. Interaction occurs between the objective task, pupils' perceptions of it, the pupils' perceptions of himself or herself as a learner, and the strategy selected. Each element has to be studied and its relationship to the others considered. If the nature of the task is misunderstood then probably an irrelevant strategy will be selected. If the strategy appears overly difficult or requiring more effort than other alternatives it will be rejected. If the learner sees himself or herself as lacking in ability or the basic prediction is that whatever is done, failure will still occur, then she or he will not be interested in examining strategies. Insufficient explanation by the teacher often inhibits the use of strategies. Winograd and Hare (1988) argue that teachers should explain *what* the strategy is; *why* it should be learned; *how* it is to be used; *when* and *where* to use it; and *how* to evaluate its use. Pupils not only have to learn how to learn, *but also need to learn how to use what they have learned.*

Not so long ago co-operation in learning was an illicit activity: now it is fostered. In fifth and sixth year revision for examinations I have long encouraged small group and partner work. Indeed, I commend it to my BEd students preparing for their examinations. In school, students make an agreement to help each other (obviously this applies to those taking the same subjects). In joint work, the first step is to write down independently, as a diagram or list of key points, everything they know about the agreed topic. Brief consultation and comparison is followed by revision where they work separately. The co-operation focuses on a 'teachback'. The old adage, 'If you want to find out whether you know something, try teaching it to someone', is employed. One partner undertakes the teachback: the recipient is far from passive; she/he corrects, raises questions, extends and elaborates, questioning helpfully. They then return to individual revision, after which roles are reversed. Teachbacks are also recorded, and played to the small group. The student who prepared it, notes the comments of the group, answering the points they raise, finally amending or adding to his or her notes.

Dansereau (1988) shows that co-operative learning allows active processing, cross-modelling and imitation. My activities, as outlined above, spur students to strive to present a model of competence to each other, introducing constructive competition into a co-operative activity. Dansereau's 'elaborative listener' uses images, mnemonics, diagrams and gives feedback on the effectiveness of the summary. If transfer of learning to other situations is desired, then the elaborative functions of the listener should be emphasised. His statement that pairs who are 'heterogeneous with regard to cognitive style and verbal ability out-perform homogeneous pairs' is arresting. Tutors could experiment, trying to find productive combinations, establishing their own criteria.

The use of tutor periods to make learning the subject of a reflective discourse – not just between teacher and students, but between student and student – reflects Lewin's view that learning is promoted when there is critical tension between concrete experience and analytic detachment. Bruner (1966) reminded us that knowledge is a process, not a product. Ideas are formed and reformed through experience: learning is also a continuous process rooted in experience and refined through analysis. Kolb (1984) takes this further, arguing that 'learning is a process of creating knowledge.' A four-step cyclical process occurs, of concrete experience, reflective observation, abstract conceptualisation and application of the concepts to new situations. Tutors will be concerned with helping pupils think about the three later stages. Before giving two activities, let me reiterate the well-known fact that the allegedly less able can think competently about learning about learning if they are given concrete, familiar and meaningful situations to consider.

An activity follows which can be used with a group of tutors. It has also proved useful as part of a training day for all staff.

Staff development: learning about learning and creating a supportive climate for it

1 The structure of this activity

1.1 The document falls into three inter-related parts:
- (i) A *general analysis* which considers the strengths and weaknesses of pupils in each year or subject group. This looks at attitudinal elements as well as specific skills.
- (ii) Exploration of the *factors within the classroom* which impinge on learning and the need to create an adaptive learning environment.
- (iii) Issues concerned with a *'whole' school policy* on learning.

1.2 Consideration will be given to peer group influences which inhibit or facilitate learning.

1.3 Parental attitudes and their positive involvement will be examined: it is not a matter solely of parental interest but how parents express their interest, and how the school uses it constructively.

2 Section one: a general analysis

2.1 Begin by filling in the simple diagram below with respect to the group for which you are concerned.

EFFECTIVE LEARNING
↑
GOAL

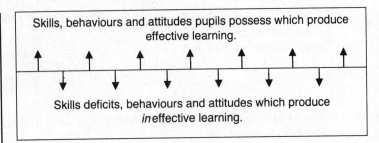

Skills, behaviours and attitudes pupils possess which produce effective learning.

Skills deficits, behaviours and attitudes which produce *in*effective learning.

(Pupils obviously differ, but you should be able to detect some general tendencies.)

2.2 Now list them in their order of importance for successful learning or the opposite.

	Factors which aid successful learning	Factors which inhibit successful learning
High ↑ ↓ Low		

Please share your ideas with a colleague, looking at them critically and examining the evidence for them. Make notes on relevant points.

2.3 Now list and examine the *attitudes* that are associated with effective learning in the pupils you teach. Compare them with the attitudes that you believe to be linked with failure in learning.

In a small group of four discuss the implications for your teaching style and classroom practice.

2.4 Anxiety needs to be looked at carefully. Girls tend to be more anxious than boys. Defences and reactions against anxiety take many forms:
- pretending that they do not care;
- procrastination about revision for examinations;
- negative comparisons of themselves with others;
- denial of the importance of the task.

(These are only a few of the possible reactions.)

In your groups discuss the impact of anxiety on the pupils you teach. It is useful to see anxiety as a signal of danger or as a reaction to threat, eg loss of face, feelings of inferiority. Look at the *situations and sources of threat*. Then look at pupils' reactions to them. Finally, consider:

- how pupils could be given the skills of dealing with anxiety in productive ways;
- which sources of anxiety could be removed or reduced in intensity.

ASK: What anxieties do teachers communicate to pupils by their attitudes and behaviours?

2.5 The image of the successful learner often lacks attraction for pupils. Even teachers at courses say, 'At the risk of appearing to be a creep . . .' Pupils are afraid of bragging or appearing to be better than their classmates. The role of successful learner sometimes brings the penalty of derision from peers.

Assess the existence of this phenomenon in your school, making notes on its form and significance. Pay especial attention to the second year which is, in the 11–16 or 11–18 school, the year in which psychological truancy appears. They are present in the flesh but absent in the spirit. Vulnerability to peer group pressures and fears of being different are strong. Make notes.

Work out ways in which there could be a planned, consistent effort by all staff to raise the acceptability of the successful learner. Go beyond encouragement in assemblies or tutor group activities to classroom interaction. Make careful notes on your approach.

---

3 Section two: Classroom interaction

3.1 Classroom interaction is concerned with the formation of the pupil's *self as a learner*. The classroom is a signal system bombarding pupils with

messages about themselves as learners;
expectations, reinforcements of certain learning
behaviours and discouragement of other
behaviours form part of interaction. Understanding
of the latent processes is crucial. Pupils may be
learning to evade demands, to give the superficial
appearance of learning, using tactics of staving off
trouble in the short run and reacting superficially.
Begin your examination by asking: what is your
model of the ideal pupil? What characteristics
would this individual possess? How does this
implicit and unacknowledged ideal pupil shape your
judgements of pupils? Discuss this in groups of
four.

3.2 A key question is: 'To what do we pay attention?'
Teachers who strongly subscribe to the belief that
pupils do things in order to get attention, actually
pay more attention to the behaviours of which they
disapprove than those they hope to induce.

Next, ask why you pay attention to those
behaviours and why you regard them as important.
What do you predict will happen if you ignore such
behaviours? Are your predictions justified? Please
make notes.

3.3 Individual praise may be unacceptable to pupils but
we can praise the group. We often neglect this.
How would you use praise to build up positive
attitudes to classroom activities and increase
pupils' *predictions* of success?

3.4 Examine:
   (i) Your style of asking questions. Teachers'
       questions inhibit learning if they over-
       emphasise factual recall or suggest that if *the*
       right answer is not produced the pupil will lose
       face. List the purposes of your questions, try-
       ing to assess the relative frequency of each
       type; assess the impact of this on pupils.
       Phillips (1980) showed that 50%+ of pupils
       aged from 9 to 14 were worried about answer-
       ing questions and making mistakes when read-
       ing aloud in class.

    (ii) Marking: it should encourage and help the learner, yet all too often it emphasises failure and the superiority of the teacher. How do you ensure your marking aids learning?

3.5 Factors which influence successful performance in the classroom include:

    (i) The pacing of the lesson. Phillips (1978) found approximately 70% of pupils experienced anxiety because the teacher went too fast for them. How do you cope with this without boring the more able pupils?

    (ii) The balance between teacher input and pupil activity. How can the most productive balance be determined?

    (iii) The teacher's skill at giving clear explanations.

    (iv) Well structured 'switch rules', i.e. instructions given when the teacher moves from 'listen to me' to 'do this'.

Discuss other aspects of classroom interaction within the control of the teacher which can be used to build pupils' confidence in themselves as learners.

3.6 Pupils' classroom attitudes and behaviours have to be scrutinised, and, where necessary, remedial steps taken. Some 'starter ideas' are set out to initiate debate.

    (i) Listening skills. The question is – for what purpose? To detect a step-by-step argument; to distinguish between fact and opinion; to pick out what is salient from what is marginal? Do they need controlled practice in developing such skills? How is this best done?

    (ii) The skills of formative assessment include development of self-evaluation, target-setting, understanding the nature of, and reasons for, a good performance in a particular subject. How would you develop them early in the secondary school?

    (iii) In a study of 55 schools, first year pupils wanted help with understanding homework instructions, the skills of doing homework and coping with the tensions produced by parents over homework. How would you work with parents on this and other matters affecting learning?

Ask why it is that in the fourth year learning is amorphous for many pupils; something you either can do or cannot do, when it should be something you can analyse and then master.

Now make your own list of the skills that you feel your pupils need to acquire. Then prepare in your group a 'one-step-at-a-time' plan for achieving this.

---

4 Section three: Developing a 'whole' school policy on learning

4.1 Thrash out what you consider to be the vital areas to be tackled.

4.2 Have you ensured that the deeper motivational aspects are being tackled, eg false stereotypes about certain subjects, and the kind of person who is good at them, false assumptions about the abilities of the sexes or areas of learned helplessness? Cite what you consider it will be essential to tackle in raising the level of performance of pupils.

4.3 How will you constructively engage with parents in this endeavour throughout the whole of their child's school career?

4.4 Assess what you hope to achieve in the next year.
Then work out carefully what you will do next term. Make your targets as clear as possible, ensuring your timing is realistic.

Topics for tutor sessions on learning might well include:

1 The development and evaluation of visual skills which are becoming increasingly important in a technological age. The reasons for their relative devaluation – let us not forget that 'non-scientists' in the sixth form tend to neglect diagrammatically and

statistically-presented information to their cost – should be assessed. Consideration should be given to ways of developing these skills in all lessons. Teachers of graphics and related subjects have much to contribute to their colleagues' teaching methods.

2 Boosting pupils' skills of developing constructive counter-arguments, backing them by rational argument and evidence. Debates in tutor periods, followed by analytic evaluation of the way arguments were refuted and justified provide a starting point. Pupils have to be as aware of process as must their teachers.

3 Examining assumptions about specific learning tasks, and learning generally in the school context.

4 The skills of evaluating evidence, and appreciating the fact that its interpretation is crucial. Acceptance of the inevitability of subjective responses to the same data.

The management of staff stress

An earlier exercise asked what calls out immature responses from individuals within the organisation. Untackled or denied stress contributes to unthinking resistance to change and abortive blame-pinning. But who cares for the carers? The answer seems to be nobody but themselves. The very commitment of teachers to the needs of pupils has caused them to deny the legitimacy of their personal and professional needs. Exhaustion and stress are recognised, but time is not allocated as a priority to tackling the sources of stress. Evidence of the dedication of teachers is found in the fact that the most frequent source of stress I meet is the feeling that they cannot do the job as well as they want to. Team work is needed to manage stress: the basic unit being the pastoral head and his or her team of tutors. Recall that pastoral activity is the pursuit of positive mental health, which means active attempts to master one's environment and a sense of achievement. Many teachers have not yet learned that if they abandon isolation and work together they have the power to change what is happening to them. Patient endurance of stress helps neither teacher nor pupils.

The skills of forward planning should be applied to the problem of modifying stress. What demands have to be met and how can we organise ourselves to meet them efficiently and economically? Clearer agreed priorities which state what must be done and what can be safely put on one side reduce pressure. Group approaches have to be applied to the problems which wear teachers down, eg the class which has learned to use passive aggression to force its teachers to take up the role of 'nag', then using what they have produced as justification for further passive resistance to teacher influence. The argument is simple: a team approach is necessary to modify the forces which exhaust by engaging us in an unending battle against apathy. Because the struggle often is, in practice, conducted individually without concerted action it is foredoomed to failure. Academic heads and pastoral heads should work together as leaders in the team approach to stress. There is room also for middle management to take a team approach to the special stresses they experience.

Two forms of provision are needed. First, there should be someone to whom the teacher suffering stress can go. If this person is to have credibility, two aspects of confidentiality have to be strictly observed:

1 *Confidentiality of access* to the source of help: those who need this support have the right to use it without colleagues knowing.
2 *Confidentiality of content* has to be resolutely observed: many teachers fear that if they are honest, this may be held against them.

There are no recipes for the provision of this support but we need to debate this in school and our professional organisations. Of one thing I am certain. Any ill-considered attempt to push the responsibility on a female deputy or senior mistress who is over-burdened will deservedly fail.

In this analysis the emphasis is on team discussion and mutual support between colleagues. Team leaders strive to create a climate of trust and safety in which tutors discuss sources of stress. This is no easy task: the culture of the school may inhibit honest discussion; whilst the implicit comparisons of oneself with others arouse defensiveness. A general approach is contained in the exercise on pages 145–50. Groups have found it useful as the initial step in team clarification of the problem. Note that the Mannheimian view of truth used in Chapter One also applies to stress. The sub-groups mentioned meet stresses peculiar to their position which are not comprehended by colleagues. Teachers of particular subjects may meet tensions not found in other subjects; the teacher of religious education, for example, may get a 'backlash' from current forms of school assemblies. For the young teacher the perception of blocked promotion coupled with impossible house prices creates a sense of futility. Knutton and Mycroft (1986) argue that teachers feel stressed when their integrity is likely to be endangered: integrity is seen as their hopes, standards, aspirations and self-image. The urgent need is to understand what different groups of staff see and experience as stressful. Also what is stressful in one school may not be so in another. Schools differ: summary statements from national surveys evoke vague recognition but greater precision and deeper analysis over a period of time is needed to assess the problem in a particular school. Earlier we saw that stress was caused by 'endless meetings which come to naught . . .' but is the stress in the 'endless meetings' or in the fact that they 'come to naught'? If both are implicated can we assess their relative contributions? Which would respond more easily to intervention? Action has been advocated, but we cannot ignore the possibility that senior and middle management stress lies in endless action which leaves no time for reflection. Group investigation of the problems could lead to recognition that unquestioned patterns of interaction exist which contribute to teacher exhaustion; the practical response is to interrupt and replace them. Priorities will have to be clarified and obligations re-examined, for example, deputy heads and pastoral heads experience conflict because their teaching and managerial or specialist activities clash. Resolute and tough-minded examination cannot be evaded.

The activity draws attention to the possibility that teacher decision making is a source of stress. Reference back to Chapter Two will be helpful. Two basic themes underlie the activity: situations are given prominence rather than personality, about which we can do little; stress is unlikely to be resolved through outside action, but considered action from within the school can control and alleviate it.

The management of teacher stress

1 The intent of this activity

1.1 To help course participants analyse the sources and nature of stresses which impinge on their professional lives.

1.2 To distinguish between stresses which can be dealt with by the individual, and those which require team-based action.

1.3 To consider the way in which classroom interaction and teacher decision making can exacerbate or alleviate the problem.

1.4 To explore the way in which problems of discipline and control contribute to loss of job satisfaction.
1.5 To consider the ways we generate some of our stresses.

2 Preparatory activities

2.1 Write down your definition of stress. Discuss it with a partner.
2.2 Why is it that some teachers suffering stress are reluctant to discuss it? Discuss in groups of four.
2.3 Evaluate this statement: One source of stress reported was, '*Endless* meetings which *come to naught.*' (Hamblin, 1989). Discuss this, focusing on the underlined words.

3 Personal professional stresses

3.1 Examine the last teaching week (Monday to Friday). List the sources of stress you experienced. Then add other stresses you can identify in your professional life, eg blocked promotion or not being able to do the job as well as you would like.
3.2 Arrange them in a *personal* hierarchy of impor- tance, ie which seem to erode your professional sense of well-being and job satisfaction most, and which have least impact? Discuss the results with another person.
3.3 The sources of stress:
    (i) Assess which stresses seem to emanate from you. Why?
    (ii) What stresses appear to stem from colleagues' attitudes and behaviours? Give the reasons for this.
    (iii) What tensions seem to be a product of teaching methods and the organisation of the school? Explain why.

3.4 A practical approach is necessary to manage and reduce stress. Two simple principles help:
   (i) See it as a 'one step at a time' activity. Begin where you are most likely to be successful.
   (ii) Be concrete and specific, not vague. Spell out exactly what you will do, eg *not* 'try to protect my lunch hour', *but* 'Go out for lunch'.
   Write out your suggestions. Then discuss as a group of six.

4   The stresses of certain groups

4.1 You have examined individual stresses, but there are also certain stresses connected with belonging to certain groups. Probationary teachers have stresses peculiar to their position: the headteacher or deputy head(s) face a different set of stress-provoking circumstances; whilst in the secondary school certain subjects seem to cause stress for those who teach them, eg religious education.
   In groups of four explore this source of stress.

4.2 It is helpful to understand the total pattern of stress within the school. Using 4.1 as a starting point, map out the *sources* and *forms* of stress in the school. Do not ignore less obvious groups such as ancillary staff. Work in groups of four and construct your map on a large sheet of paper. Then compare it with that of another small group, explaining and justifying what you have done.

4.3 On large sheets of paper list ideas for modifying two of the stresses you have identified. Be practical. Also look at the 'costs' of the proposed action.
   In groups of six share ideas: build on them in preparation for developing a whole policy on managing stress.

5 Examining classroom interaction and teacher decision making

5.1 Explore the sources of tension within the classroom. List them.

5.2 Then examine the general level of classroom management in the school. Look more specifically at:
   (i) teachers' skills of defusing situations;
   (ii) methods of coping with pupils who invite confrontation;
   (iii) what some teachers make stronger as they interact with a class. Are they reinforcing positive or negative behaviours?

5.3 Now explore the nature of decision making by the teacher, and its relationship to teacher stress. Recall that teacher decision making becomes automatic: it is therefore rarely examined although it is sometimes responsible for stress. Explore the following:
   (i) the decisions made by the teacher before the lesson, eg the level of noise that will be tolerated. How could they contribute to success or stress? If they seem to be related to stress, what help should be given, and by whom?
   (ii) Decision making in class is about the following (amongst other things):
     • To what do we pay attention?
     • What do we *predict* will happen if we ignore it?
     • What do we believe to be an effective way of coping?
Extend your analysis to as many aspects of classroom interaction as you can. Assess links with stress and suggest remedial action. Make notes.

5.4 Consider the elements of teacher decision making which lead to confrontations with:
   (i) pupils;
   (ii) parents;

(iii) colleagues.
What could be done to rectify this?

---

6 Discipline and stress

6.1 Ineffective punishment and conflicts among staff about school rules exacerbate stress. Teachers become worn out by administering ineffective reprimands in some schools. Schools which foster teacher stress are often marked by the cry, 'We've tried being hard; we've tried being soft; nothing works; what now?'
 Discuss and suggest a policy for:
  (i) ensuring a consistent policy on the keeping of school rules;
  (ii) making parents aware of the way their attitudes and behaviour influence pupils' attitudes to learning and keeping school rules;
  (iii) helping parents see the need for, and giving them the skills of, supporting the work of the teacher.
 Make practical suggestions for achieving the above in groups of four.

6.2 Discuss
  (i) What do you see as the most common offences in your school?
  (ii) How effective are the punishments or other measures taken in response to the offences?
  (iii) What do pupils see as punishment?
  (iv) What disagreements and inconsistencies exist among staff about discipline.
  (v) Assess the way in which a more productive approach can be taken to these matters.

---

7 A 'whole' school strategy for managing stress

7.1 In groups of eight begin to prepare a plan for

> reducing staff stress in your school, and for managing that which cannot be eliminated.
>   (i) Incorporate a clear indication of priorities.
>   (ii) Indicate any necessary prerequisites, eg a survey within the school of stress or parental contact.
> 7.2 Distinguish between factors which could be dealt with by:
>   (i) individual action or support;
>   (ii) organised team work.
>   Pay special attention to the need to take planned team interventions to the problems which beset teachers, eg a class which habitually uses passive aggression against teachers.
> 7.3 As you develop your plan ask, 'What is the balance between the preventive, and the remedial?' Are you paying sufficient attention to the former?
> 7.4 Meet another group and explain your strategy to them, asking for constructive appraisal.

The teacher works within an anxiety-provoking context. Heads of year or house should provide tutors with basic understanding of anxiety. Sound discussions are found (see, for example, Ruebush, 1963; Lazarus, 1966; and Spielberger (ed.), 1966). Buss (1980) provides a stimulating account of social anxieties. Anxiety is more than an unpleasant state of unease: as Lazarus (1966) shows, it is a signal of danger or a response to a threat perceived by the individual. Rogers (1959) believes that anxiety is due to discrepancy between the individual's concept of herself or himself and experience which violates self-worth. Even if perception of the experience is distorted, threat is still felt, and the helper has to take it seriously. Lazarus highlights threat as the key to understanding anxiety. The threat we meet is that there 'is too much to cope with' and the response is, at the extremes, feverish activity or withdrawal into inertia. In her study of depression, Rowe (1978) shows how individuals who are severely depressed build around themselves walls of language structures composed of propositions which inhibit interaction with others. They then see themselves as 'being cut off from and as choosing to be cut off from interaction with others ...' Obviously such cases need specialist treatment. To meddle is to invite trouble, but we should be aware that stress produces a sense of isolation which the victim may promote actively.

Threat, real or imagined, accurately or distortedly perceived, is therefore the object of action in working on our own, and others', stresses. A helpful distinction is between *trait* and *state* anxiety. The former refers to what we mean by an 'anxious person'. It is the extent to which someone has a predisposition to respond to many situations with anxiety. The intensity of their response would also be considered to be disproportionate to the reality of the threat by most people. He or she sees a wide range of situations not usually considered to be threatening as potentially harmful. Colleagues suffering from trait anxiety may develop rigid and sometimes self-punishing defences, such as a limited set of 'safe' behaviours which do not accommodate new demands, avoidance of certain situations or negative black humour. Pastoral heads alerted to trait anxiety can avoid threatening them further and proffer support.

State anxiety derives from the threat generated by situations, such as examinations, job interviews, leadership, coping with a paranoid parent or the prospect of a major operation. Little can be done about trait anxiety *as such* due to its origins in personality or constitutional factors, but we can help colleagues cope better with anxiety-provoking situations.

The distinction is best seen as a practical one, and as a safety-line which prevents the helper getting out of depth. It conceals conceptual and technical complications which the interested may wish to investigate. Trait anxiety is concerned with the assessment of stable individual differences with regard to a relatively permanent, and apparently unitary, personality characteristic. But it includes proneness to guilt, embarrassment and suspiciousness which may be enhanced by personal circumstances and the nature of teaching. Neurological factors, body chemistry and long-standing conditioning may be inextricably intertwined. This suffices to warn against easy attribution of causation, and shows the need to deal with the situation. The helper can, however, orientate to the problem by asking whether perception of the threat can be reasonably described as realistic or unrealistic, and whether it is primarily located in the environment or the individual's inner life.

In helping tutors understand and cope with stress and its concomitant, anxiety, they need to evaluate their life space. The conscientious teacher experiences more obvious stress. Over-investment in school life with consequent narrowing of outside satisfactions makes job stress more damaging than when compensatory satisfaction and reward exist elsewhere. There comes the point, however, especially for senior and middle management, when job stress threatens or sours other aspects of life creating a disquieting insecurity or even loss of identity. Rational discussion of such things is essential staff development. Understanding stress in oneself and others means that the basic mechanisms of interaction have to be explored:

1 Predictions, and the way they shape behaviour, have been mentioned. Under stress, unrealistically negative predictions cause us to behave in ways which call out rejection by others, or create complicated tensions. We then become trapped in what we have created, and because it is our creation, we find it difficult to find a way out.
2 Comparisons seem an inescapable part of school life. The stressed compare themselves in a denigrating way with others. Thoughtless comparisons and judgements by those not suffering from stress increase distress.
3 Teachers are conscientious, but a minority have unrealistic ideal-selves as teachers which would be impossible for even a saint to achieve. Harsh self-condemnation then makes them difficult colleagues.
4 Some stressed individuals feel that they are the victims of expectations of others which erode their competence or deny their values.
5 Stress calls out less-than-admirable tendencies. Suspicion grows, accompanied by the desire to hit out. We then see others as possessing negative motives and being ill-disposed towards us.

All this is highly subjective, but so is stress! Heads of year or house will have to work out carefully the way they will broach these issues with tutors. Those who see their roles in limited ways may see it as an impossible task and become defensive. Yet where it has been attempted the response of tutors has been warmly appreciative – the pastoral head has greater credibility as a caring figure. Simple activities yield worthwhile results. In courses I have presented this:

> 'Recall a period or situation when you were under stress. Assess what happened to your perceptions of people involved in the stress situation. How did you view yourself?'

Next, they are asked to consider their feelings about these statements:

'I can't take any more.'
'I know they think I can't cope.'
'Then I feel helpless.'
'I know I ought to get a grip on things: I'm ashamed of myself.'

Then in small groups they discuss accepting responses to these remarks.

Such simple activities, undertaken in a climate of support, produce realisation of the shallowness of conventional responses to the expression of stress, and reinforce the professional legitimacy of caring for one another. We endorse the primacy of listening in counselling, but have we learned to listen to one another?

The ideas which follow have been used in group work and individually with stressed teachers. Pastoral heads will have to adapt them for their own use. Management of stress within the school must be seen as a process which occurs gradually. Initial explorations move into a 'take off' situation where results begin to appear. The time element is unpredictable. Some schools seem able to incorporate the findings and modify stress-producing factors fairly quickly, others experience difficulty. The culture of the school seems to be the influential factor. It is easy to say, 'One step at a time', but harder to tolerate this in practice. The aim is to build on strengths rather than solely attack weaknesses. Sensible people begin with the situations where something can be achieved rather than instantly homing in on the most intractable element. Individuals also gain a sense of control by analysing problems and constructing a hierarchy of difficulty, tackling the less intimidating elements first. The aim is to replace amorphousness by a structure which encourages problem solving.

For individuals and groups, diagrams and precise questions break into what Ivey (1986) calls 'errors of causation, distortion, over-generalisation'. Counselling has always been concerned with the present, but recognises that the present partially consists of repeating mistakes from the past. Examples are:

1 In which situations do you experience strong feelings of stress, and in which do you feel free of it? What are the differences between them?
2 What triggers off the feelings of tension?
3 How do you usually cope with stress?
4 Explain what happened the last time you experienced severe stress.

5 Do the expectations of colleagues (or pupils) play an important part in producing stress?

Simple life-space diagrams, as described by Hamblin (1974) can be used. The mapping technique is also productive. Through such simple devices a frame is developed within which things fall into perspective. Controlled self-observation can be used as part of stress management. Groups and individuals are asked to observe themselves. Triggers for stress, periods of vulnerability are detected, and measures for coping are devised. The sense of being able to experiment with behaviours is vital in restoring or strengthening the sense of efficacy. Verbalising plans for combating stress break into the resigned inertia or the compulsive frenetic activity which seem to be the hallmarks of stress. If situations are seen as immutable then we are not motivated to act.

Let us look a little more closely at the ways individuals respond to stress, remembering that what is true for the individual is also relevant to the group. Shared definitions of the nature of, and reasons for, stress exist within a school. Lazarus (1966) accepts that the transactions between the individual and his or her environment are the crucial points for intervention. Most counselling theories of the behavioural type also incorporate this. Two types of appraisal form the crux of Lazarus' work:

1 *Primary appraisal* is identification of the exact nature and location of what is seen as threat. Once this has been done, the helper, whilst accepting the individual's perceptions, works out with them sources of help or countervailing features. Anxiety causes rigidity: the extremely anxious person concentrates solely on the harmful, denying themselves the possibility of change. A caution: credibility is lost by insensitive probing. Well-intentioned but clumsy action may stimulate near panic. Yet clarification is indispensable because ambiguity amplifies anxiety. Intuitive assessment – checked against the evidence as soon as possible – of the stressed person's deep-seated beliefs of the source of control allows sensible adaptation by the supporter. Do they see control as largely residing in themselves or in their environment? If the latter, then they may take a reactive position, rejecting responsibility for their contribution to their plight, and predicting that nothing will work. Intense subscription to the former may call out harsh self-condemnation and guilt. The 'ought' compounds the emotional turmoil. Bringing such mechanisms to the forefront is as vital as coping with the obvious sources of stress. Adaptation means giving the externally controlled a clear-cut plan for action and sharp

definition of each step to be taken. Primary appraisal functions to prevent concentration on the anxiety to the neglect of what causes it.

2 *Secondary appraisal* assesses the effectiveness and costs of coping with the threat. Coping may be effective but too costly. Lazarus (1966) and Endler *et al* (1962) demonstrate that individual differences in susceptibility to anxiety are of less importance than perceptions of the situation, and crucially the method of coping. This is a hopeful position, because we can do something about perceptions and behaviour. Examination of coping mechanisms may reveal that they make matters worse, may be primitive or produce guilt. Examples of such reactions are attack or displacing aggression on to those not implicated – pupils or a spouse. Examination is followed by just enough recasting of beliefs about what will, or will not, work; what is proper or inappropriate behaviour for a professional; and what will be the likely responses of others to attempted change to allow unfreezing of compulsive activity patterns. (Tyler's minimum change therapy is very useful!) Efforts at support must extend self-respect: counselling accepts that self-respect is essential for responsible behaviour.

Counselling includes confrontation which is not aggressive in nature or intent. Reflection on the discrepancies between what people say (indeed believe) they do, and what they actually do, is helpful confrontation. Stressed people haphazardly fall into Orwellian 'double-think', saying contradictory things in different settings or groups. Tensions and insecurity then grow, keeping their different 'faces' absorbs energy, yet they seem not to comprehend why. Some version of the incident analysis (Hamblin, 1984, p 230) or the exercise derived from the work of Argyis will help the stressed cope with self-deceptive behaviours. Dramatisation has to be guarded against. Stress brings out people's latent capacity for amplifying emotions. One's response is to be reassuringly down-to-earth while guarding against dismissiveness.

The major push of heads of house or year should be towards prevention. The general group approach to stress management includes examination of decision making, which was discussed in Chapter Two. Tutors should raise their level of understanding of the behaviours and intent of pupils who present difficulties in class. Guidance can be obtained from Cohen and Cohen (1987), Coulby and Harper (1985), Topping (1983) and Watkins and Wagner (1987). This becomes more, not less, urgent as pupils are given greater autonomy in classroom learning. Situations, rather than personality, have to be studied: making personality the hub leaves us helpless; analysis of situations suggests times of action. Pastoral heads' best contribution to stress management may well be concerted effort in helping tutors to:

- read situations accurately;
- intelligently anticipate the course of events;
- take positive early action in situations spelling trouble;
- effectively defuse confrontations.

Observational and diagnostic skills are needed by tutors. Changes in peer group membership, early recognition of attitudinal change or signals of dissociation from the values and objectives of the school have to be registered and grappled with as early as possible. I suspect that a great deal of tension in teachers could be dissipated by a team attack on the psychological truancy which appears in the second year. We have to learn how to reinforce a positive group identity for a class. Simple measures work when *consistently applied*. Delinquency has been linked with inconsistent discipline at home: today, it may be matched by inconsistent discipline at school. Certain pupils energetically and skilfully exploit this.

A whole-school policy on positive discipline

1 Objectives

1.1 To consider the topic in the context of school development rather than as a problem to be studied in isolation.

1.2 To distinguish between punishment and discipline: searching for ways of reinforcing self-discipline and students' sense of responsibility for their behaviours.

1.3 To examine the system-based factors which push students towards affiliation with the school or cause them to dissociate from its values.

1.4 To examine measures which involve students actively in authority relations and build up perceptions of the school as a caring community.

1.5 To consider ways in which students can participate

in the formulation, evaluation and modification of school rules.

---

2 Preliminary orienting questions

2.1 Is order in school largely dependent on the presence of punishment or are there factors which are more important, such as:
  (i) the quality of staff–student relationships;
  (ii) the general level of teachers' skills of classroom management.
2.2 Is punishment a necessary deterrent at times, but a practice which has little positive educative value?
2.3 In your working groups list what you consider to be the *justifiable* objectives of a 'whole' school policy on positive discipline.
Share ideas with another working group.

---

3 An armchair diagnosis

(This should be followed up by action research in the school.)

3.1 What are the most common offences in your school?
3.2 How effective are the punishments and other steps taken in reponse to them?
3.3 What do students see as effective punishment? Do their views coincide with those of staff?
3.4 What do students see as just or unjust punishment?
3.5 What disagreements and inconsistencies exist among staff about discipline? Is there a possibility that students perceive and exploit them?

4 Classroom interaction and positive discipline

(This section takes the view that students' classroom behaviours are the main area of concern for the teacher. Classroom rules may have to be negotiated with students, but other factors outlined below have to be studied.)

4.1 What are students' perceptions of an effective and fair teacher? Work recently undertaken in a Midland school showed pupils valued the teacher's willingness to explain, to give instructions clearly, and to encourage rather than cause the pupils to 'lose face' with peers. Other studies stress evidence of preparation, and the skills of managing activities so that pupils understand what is required of them.

4.2 Classroom rules have to be considered and negotiated.

(i) A first step may be consideration of the teacher's idiosyncratic classroom rules about level of noise, permission-seeking and movement.

(ii) Rules about pupil–pupil interaction have to be established after discussion with pupils. (There is some evidence that pupils approve of punishment given to a pupil for being unkind to someone.)

(iii) Rules about teacher–pupil interaction should be examined. Negotiation should show that the rules are as binding on the teacher as they are on the pupil!

(iv) Rules about situations of danger, eg at the swimming bath or in workshops or laboratories need to be especially clear, and possibly draw more on the teacher's awareness of contingencies.

4.3 How would you as a staff begin negotiation with students on classroom rules? It will have to be seen as a process over time incorporating a step-by-step approach. Hasty action is to be avoided: students acquire attitudes and skills gradually.

4.4 Parallel to the negotiation is a need for the teacher to evaluate her or his largely automatic decision-making style. Unquestioned decisions often produce friction and difficulties.

   (i) Decisions made before class about the noise level that will be tolerated, the pace of the lesson, the balance between teacher input and student activity become habitual, and are not subjected to rigorous scrutiny. Because they are inappropriate for a particular class, unnecessary tensions then arise.

   (ii) Decisions are made almost unconsciously in face of the pressures of classroom life. A 'whole' school policy on discipline requires us to assess:

   – To what do we pay attention? Why?
   – What do we predict will happen if we do not pay attention to it?
   – What do we predict will be an effective reaction? Is our belief justified?

In the working group, assess how you would undertake investigation into decision-making and other aspects of classroom interaction, eg expectations of certain students or small groups of students.

---

5 Pupil participation in the development of a whole-school policy on positive discipline

5.1 Discipline should be seen as part of strengthening the concept of the school as a community in which two sources of identity are developed:

   (i) The security which comes from belonging to a community in which one is cared for and respected.

   (ii) The development of self-awareness and responsible identity based on the challenges offered by curricular and pastoral work.

5.2 How will pupils be involved systematically and responsibly in authority relationships?

(They were involved as prefects etc in the primary school)

(i)   Is there a place for prefects in each year?

(ii) How will you ensure that as many individuals as possible play an active part in maintaining authority? Prefects could, for example, be changed termly.

(iii) What part could the sixth or fifth year students play in supporting the system, and providing younger students with models of competence?

(iv) If this development was to be introduced, what would be the best way of doing it? Bottom up or top down, ie begin with the first year and work up or move from the fifth year downwards? There are advantages and disadvantages in both.

5.3 Even more important is the conscious creation of a network of helping relationships *within* a particular age group and *between* different age groups. Sixth form students already act as helpers in many schools, but this can be extended with profit as work in some schools has demonstrated.

Is there a place for this in your school? If so, work out your strategy for developing it. Pay careful attention to the initial stages as they determine later success or failure.

---

6 The contribution of the pastoral programme

6.1 The pastoral programme should function to reinforce achievement and help pupils acquire crucial skills.

6.2 Assess the topics and skills that you feel the pastoral programme should include to support the school policy on discipline.

6.3 The skills might include systematic development of standpoint taking, ie seeing matters from the perspective of others, decision-making in

problematic situations, assessing the consequences and costs of different courses of action,
understanding the nature and functions of authority
and the nature of justice in social interaction.

Co-operation should be an integral part of
pastoral work. Consider the possibility of a goal
being set for a whole year, eg a project which
would benefit the whole school. All tutor groups
work together to achieve this end. Pupils have the
experience of seeing tutors actively collaborating.
Evaluate the possibility of such activities operating
in your school to support discipline.

---

7 Concluding points

7.1 Consistency is essential to provide the sense of
security necessary for positive discipline in
adolescence. This is not the same as rigidity, in
which all pupils are treated identically. A 'tariff'
approach – 'Do this, and you pay that' – inhibits
moral development. The pastoral programme
should encourage pupils to consider the concepts
of need, intent, self-respect and compassion as
part of taking a mature attitude to punishment. A
positive approach to discipline is part of the
school's endeavour to create the truly morally
educated person in an age of accelerating change
and an increasingly multi-cultural society.

7.2 Research into punishment suggest that it is usually
only effective when administered in a context of
liking and respect.

Even this simple activity opens doors for action. Unless we search
out pupils' views of effective punishment, understand what they
regard as just or unjust, and help them develop mature views of
authority, abortive punishments will remain the norm in pastoral
work. If staff disagreements about the purpose and nature of
discipline are brushed to the side or seen as too explosive for

discussion, the web of contradictions will inhibit the development of both responsible individuality and a caring community.

Tutors need help with the skills of defusing situations, otherwise they escalate and energy is used up in remedying what need not have happened. Simple points include:

1 Preventing the pupil locking one into a confrontation to which the rest of the class is the audience. The situation has to be changed. Opening a window, sending someone reliable on a message or errand, praising the class or paying some positive attention to them interrupts the sequence of events the troublesome pupil hopes to develop, and divests him of the audience.
2 Pitch and volume of voice should be kept under control. A rise in pitch automatically evokes further tension.
3 Eye contact should be used carefully. It can be confrontational and reinstate the situation described in 1. Girls are especially sensitive to eye contact which savours of 'staring me out'.
4 Breach of personal space is always to be avoided if the pupil is in a state of arousal. The rough guide is to stay an arm's length plus a wrist and hand away.
5 Avoid any public challenge, eg 'I expect you to do it within the next five minutes.'

The strategy is withdrawal with dignity, giving the pupil the opportunity to recover his or her balance. Rationality can then resume its place in interaction. It is surprising that these basic suggestions inevitably launch groups into thoughtful discussion. As follow-up, pastoral heads will find it useful to initiate discussion of ways in which tutors' activities could help pupils deal responsibly with frustration, loss of face and peer group pressures which contribute to misbehaviour. (Further discussion can be found in Hamblin, 1984.)

Management of stress is essential. Although the individual's stress has to be met with compassion, it is through system-based approaches that stress will be controlled. Management of time and the development of team approaches to difficulties form the basis for planned preventive work. Team approaches to the modification of difficult classes (see Hamblin, 1980, 1984) are necessary.

Coping with conflicting expectations

Stress is not solely located in the individual: it is embedded in the context in which the person works. The 'Mannheimian view of truth' illustrated in Chapter One shows that pastoral heads have to function in a setting of conflicting expectations. Middle management occupies a pivotal position between the class teacher and senior management; both groups attributing motives, making judgements, and hoping to manipulate the head of year or house in furtherance of their own purposes. *Manipulate* as used here means the attempt to control through various sources of influence.

1 Working as a group, pastoral heads should specify as concretely as possible the expectations of them held by:
- class teachers;
- senior management.

2 They then assess each group's expectations as:
- realistic/unrealistic;
- helpful/unhelpful;
- desirable/undesirable;
- positive/negative.

Considerable debate then takes place about the significance of the assessments. Groups often add their own bipolar dimensions.

3 The next step is to examine the contradictions between:
- the two groups' expectations;
- their own interpretations of their role and those of each group.

4 After this, the discrepancies are graded according to the amount of stress they produce.

5 Decisions are then made about the initiation of negotiation: obviously the team will keep the need to extend their credibility in mind. A clumsy attack on the most important issue, and consequent failure in negotiation, will take months of determined effort to repair.

In assessing the significance of colleagues' expectations, the wider context of probabilities and predictions has to be taken into account. The current, and unnecessary, devaluation of teachers, the feared constraints of the National Curriculum, and the possible erosion of the professionalism of teachers through changes in training and entry, impinge on expectations and relationships between groups to provoke stress.

Note that the analysis should also be conducted laterally. Relations between academic heads and pastoral heads contribute to stress on both sides.

Key incidents

Pastoral heads face a continuous flow of events: pressure of time prevents them from analysing those which seem to be particularly exhausting or repetitive. Better management of them will reduce stress. They can be examined through the *incident analysis* below, taken from Hamblin (1984), *Pastoral Care: A Training Manual*:

Incident analysis: basic questions

1 What was the intent of participants? What possibilities for conflict or co-operation existed?
2 Which aspects of roles became salient? What justifications for their positions were held by participants? What beliefs about authority and ways of behaving in this situation were present?
3 What frustrations came into being?
4 How was communication affected by participants' perceptions of each others' motives?
5 What blocks to a positive outcome were present? What facilitated a successful outcome?
6 What priorities were held by participants – helpfully or unhelpfully?
7 Who constituted the 'invisible audience'? Whose later judgements had to be kept in mind?
8 What were the implications of the outcome for future interaction?
9 How could the handling of similar incidents be improved?

A team approach to the different views and perspectives of such events develops from the analysis. Stressful contradictions and responses which negate one another can be eliminated, and a consistent approach substituted.

5 Interviewing skills, self-evaluation and staff appraisal

The intent of this chapter

We now return to the skills pastoral heads *as a team* need to develop if they are to contribute to the integration of the sub-populations which make up the secondary school. The need is urgent: we delude ourselves if we feel that it is confined to the few disorganised or mismanaged schools. Within the last week I have worked with the staff of an excellent school. Commitment was high: yet there was evidence of misperception of the nature of demands of a competent and caring senior management; mutual failure to recognise sources of stress for the other group was present. Highly dedicated teachers had not grasped the way in which their situational perspective, and subtle – probably only partially apprehended – group affiliations blunted their honest endeavour to change productively. The question of how we change these self-defeating processes will not be answered by this book. It can, however, illuminate the problem, and encourage pastoral teams to think of ways and means of initiating change.

If resistance to change is to be overcome, and desired change made a reality, pastoral heads must learn to employ the technique of self-evaluation constructively. They must also understand the anxiety-provoking, although potentially rewarding, process of staff appraisal. More intimidatingly, they must be prepared to play a considered role in it. A first step will be acquiring the skills of depth interviewing, which embodies counselling techniques. One member of the pastoral middle management should also set out to acquire expertise in the theory and practice of attitude change. It is imperative that, as more complex and important judgements are demanded from teachers, which they will have to justify, and for which they will be accountable, this person gains understanding of the perceptual and cognitive processes which shape judgements and guide our actions. This is not asking for amateur psychologists, but for understanding of what is at the heart of curriculum and pastoral development.

Interviewing

In discussing careers HMI (1988) define counselling as a 'purposeful relationship which helps individuals to understand and cope more effectively with themselves and their circumstances, and to handle their personal development, their roles and relationships with others'. This makes an excellent orientation to the interviewing that pastoral heads should be doing. Formative assessment in the secondary school applies to teachers as much as to students. Understanding the dynamics of the interview is crucial if it is not to be damaging to both parties. Insecurity could turn the interview into mutual collusion where reality is denied. Interviewing both colleagues and pupils requires firm, helpful coping with tendencies to 'keep face', attempted evasion of distasteful facts, anger, distrust, anxiety about status, and emotional blackmail on both sides. Without this, the self-evaluation or appraisal interview will be anodyne or a shared flight from reality.

The interview, as much as counselling, is a disciplined process in which the onus is on the interviewer to understand and control herself or himself and assess the impact of his or her actions on the interviewee. Banaka (1971) demonstrates that the interviewer has to be aware of her or his feelings to prevent unwitting prejudice, distortion of meaning, or imposition of his or her viewpoint on the other. Most of us are aware that the interview can be contaminated by associations of trouble for pupils. Defensive reactions are stimulated very easily: but have we given sufficient thought about these possibilities in interviews with colleagues? Clumsy questions and failure to adapt the interviewing style to the interviewee creates a climate of interrogation to which colleagues respond by superficial acquiescence which masks resentment, later expressed in the staff-room or the secure environment provided by a supportive group of friends who then devalue the interview. Probing may provoke an upsurge of emotion in those who feel stressed or unable to tolerate one more demand. The released anger is not necessarily therapeutic: even if it has benefits for the individual, others may exploit it for their own purposes. Rumours of manipulation or 'doing things' to interviewees circulate, gaining credence in the process.

It is crucial that interviewers should practice systematically ways of coping with unexpected difficulties or the sudden revelation of deep feelings. Helpful videotapes exist – such as the Somerset ones (1988) – but they may over-stress rationality. Not every appraisal interview will be the urbane, civilised and co-operative affair that some tapes suggest. Equally, it is unhelpful to over-stress the difficulties. In training it is sensible to anticipate problems and show ways of coping without suggesting they are inevitable.

A simple framework for training is:

1 *Preparation for the interview*
Heads of year or house should consider how they will prepare themselves and how the interviewee should approach the interview. Both need to orientate themselves and marshal their strategies.

- What is the main purpose of the interview? Clarification and formulation of a problem in ways which make it amenable to intervention? Understanding a situation more accurately? Setting mutually-agreed targets?
- What information is possessed about the interviewee? How precise and reliable is it? Is it likely to influence one's perceptions – perhaps because it is emotive – or trigger off unquestioned assumptions?
- Is the interviewer's existing relationship with the interviewee neutral, positive or negative? The latter may arouse unwarranted suspicion, whilst friendship brings the danger of over-estimating the extent of agreement (Sears and Whiting; 1973).
- Preliminary evaluation of the following will help the interviewer use the time to best advantage.

    (i) the changes necessary in the interviewee and others: problems do not exist in a vacuum!
    (ii) the interviewee's potential for achieving the probable goals;
    (iii) what would hinder or help her or him in the task?

    Anticipation should not, however, become a self-fulfilling prophecy or restrict action.
- Standpoint-taking can usefully be exercised before the interview. Ask what the interviewee is likely to see as your intent, and

what might motivate her or him to distort or conceal information, or co-operate with you. The obvious fact that participation is influenced by perceptions of the interviewer and the likely outcomes is strangely ignored in practice.

2   *The interview*

Counselling principles and techniques yield results. Remember that counselling helps people find out how they defeat themselves or are defeated. But as this is achieved we never remove the responsibility from the individual.

- A basic question for formative assessment interviews is 'How do I create an atmosphere of rapport without compromising myself?' Immediate signals of acceptance and respect are essential. In assessing the time to be allowed, a few minutes should be allocated for this. An inexperienced or insecure interviewer plunges in immediately. Some find it difficult to move from initial creation of rapport to the business of the interview. The reasons for this have to be brought into the open. What is the threat, or is it incompetence?
- Interaction will include activity in which both participants make notes or diagrams. It is not confined to the verbal. Most important is the requirement that one should be concrete and specific, looking at the costs and consequences of possible courses of action. The old, although far from mundane, approach of, 'Where are you now?' and 'Where would you like to be?' can be effective if the interviewer:

  (i)   helps the person clarify priorities;
  (ii) encourages a step-by-step approach to dealing with a situation;
  (iii) identifies what might hamper coping, encouraging the interviewee to work out for himself or herself ways of dealing with it.

Goals must be clearly defined and accepted by the interviewee before time is invested in determining the steps that lead to goal achievement. So self-evident, that its mention seems banal! Yet on many occasions I have seen counsellors spend time and energy abortively because they have ignored what seems so obvious.

The interviewer needs to be alert to discrepancies and

confusions in the interviewee's statements, of which she or he is unaware. They have to be brought resolutely to the forefront without losing sight of the vulnerability or defensiveness of the other. Clarification, not condemnation, is the aim.

- Summarising at intervals is a key skill. It is not confined solely to the end of the interview. Used judiciously, it clarifies and leads into the next stage. Summaries distinguish between feelings, opinions and facts, allowing the person to assess and select a course of action for detailed exploration. Two dangers exist. The interviewer may swamp the other with suggestions, making decisions unnecessarily difficult, or he or she may convey expectations in a manner difficult to resist. Interviewees read cues more avidly than we realise, and then conform to them. Strong expectations emanate from both sides. The interviewer is in danger of being coerced emotionally into meeting them.

- Tyler (1969) says that interview information must be accurate and free from bias. Emotive stereotypes have seductive appeal, eg 'restoring and protecting our traditional standards'. Bias may enter because the role relationships of interviewer and interviewee elsewhere contain elements of dependency, obligation or power.

3 *Ending and following up interviews*

An interviewee should leave feeling that something worthwhile has been achieved. Gains must be specified, eg increased clarity about a problem, a sense of direction or targets to be achieved. If action has to be taken, the last section of the interview not only includes clear specification of the means but also anticipation of potential hazards. Ways of avoiding or dealing with risks should be worked out. Supports and measures for ensuring that recommendations are carried out must be clear to all concerned. (Further discussion of these points occurs in the section on staff appraisal.)

Pacing requires sensitive adaptation by the interviewer. One can push too hard. If tension or threat has not been resolved – at least openly acknowledged – before the evaluation element of an interview is reached, then hostility and evasion occur. Cues such as hesitations, silences or changes of topic should be noted. Foot-tapping or pushing the chair further away from the interviewer can be significant. Interviewing is based on balancing acts. Adjusting the pace to the interviewee has to be weighed against achieving the objectives in the time available. It could be disquieting for both individuals if time runs out, and the summary which highlights the fact that a purposeful experience has occurred cannot be given. Logical sequence of topics has to be balanced against the ability to face facts without over-reactions. To rush into emotionally-charged areas invites resistance and anger. Yet to delay may cause apprehension and increase threat. It is tempting to say we must rely on intuition: perhaps sensitivity to low-level signals and coding our messages precisely is better. Certainly we must check intuitions: they can deceive us.

Rigid assumptions about the role of the interviewer must be questioned. Formative assessment requires the interviewer to recognise that different styles will be needed with different people. Formative interviewing is a process, not an event. The interviewer changes his or her style to match what is happening. Greater support, even tolerance of dependency may be essential at first; challenge and positive confrontation later. This is not inconsistency. Consistency comes from the purposive relationship with the interviewee; the ability to relate one's actions to the desired outcomes, coupled with honest explanation, and justification of one's approach. There is no right approach and no room for omnipotence or seduction. The principles of concern and self-discipline apply always to the inter-viewer. We select the behaviour which we believe will be helpful to keep the process moving.

Interviews embodying a counselling process can legitimately include:

1 *Advising* – where the individual is helped to detect (or is shown, if necessary) possible courses of action, and then encouraged to evaluate them. Conversely, the interviewer occasionally has the ethical responsibility to show that one line of action only is in the interviewee's best interests. Advice as an opinion about future action should only be given after the situation has clarified, and must be put forward tentatively, except in extremely urgent situations.

2 *Aiding communication* includes active listening and keeping a sharp eye on the impact and intent of our comments. Repeating phrases, especially those which seem emotionally loaded, encourages the interviewee to assess and clarify. This does not endorse saying, 'What you mean is ...'. Suggestions will, as usual, be phrased tentatively. Detection of ambiguities and unacknowledged

contradictions, rather than creating a climate of compliance, should be our aim.

3 *Supporting* must be employed with care. Statements such as 'That seems a productive line of attack' or 'That's excellent' may boost confidence, but they can be smugly patronising, or unwitting selective shaping of the course of action. Helping the individual identify sources of support or determine how she or he will mobilise resources to achieve the goal keeps the responsibility with them.

4 *Teaching* has a place. Presenting an appropriate model of decision making or problem solving within which the interviewee examines the problem can empower him or her.

5 *Exploring alternatives* is to be stressed. Students or colleagues can be stimulated to test in imagination a line of action, anticipating snags and assessing likely benefits. They then discard the plan; extend or adapt it; and proceed to implement it. Formative assessment requires the person to try new strategies in an open-minded way.

Interviewing which incorporates a counselling element stresses adaptation through the use of a variety of techniques. Let me illustrate this by considering pupils. Those whose preferred way of learning is largely visual or active, obviously respond better to interviews where drawings and diagrams are used, particularly if they can be involved in their production (see Hamblin, 1974 and 1978). Pupils who experience difficulty in assessing themselves react positively when they can compare themselves with a concrete model of behaviour – 'This is how somebody of your age tackled the problem or felt about this situation'. Formative assessment is about means/ends thinking but that does not imply we always work from the present to the future state of affairs. Some pupils prefer to work back from the desired future to the present.

Productive formative assessment and interviewing stresses the concrete and specific. We help the interviewee analyse the last time they lost control, experienced stress or failed in a learning task. Heads of year or house, as much as tutors, need to refine their observational skills. Not only must they be employed in assessing signs of teacher stress, or pupils' deterioration in standard of dress, level of confidence, or evasion of contact with teachers, and changed peer group interaction, they must also be given a prime place in interviewing. Suppressed anger, unease and anxiety should be noted, and brought into the open without creating guilt or sparking off conflict. Reading low-level cues without prejudging their significance is crucial for effective interviewing. One also observes the transition from topic to topic, asking why it occurs in that particular way. Is it because the interviewee has exhausted the point; have disturbing implications been apprehended; or has confidence to talk about something vital been acquired? The interviewer is tested out by the interviewee who would be naïve to trust blindly. If we are seen as rigidly judgemental, incompetent, or dismissive, then the interviewee has to shift his ground and talk about something innocuous. Never forget that as interviewers we may be seen as incompetent or authoritarian, therefore the interviewee defends herself or himself by change of topic.

Middle-management exploration of interviewing should give weight to apparently less practical, yet vital issues. Sensitivity to what are emotive words and ideas for the interviewee allow perception of confusions, recognition of less obvious confusions and contradictions. Pastoral heads should ask why, and when, opinions and feelings need to be given primacy. When are precise facts essential? Interviewing may become a process of bargaining, sometimes implicit. If so, what is it about, and what are the intended gains of the participants? Can this bargaining assume greater importance than the avowed purposes of the interview? What aspects of role in a particular interview are likely to become salient? Role as officially prescribed, as expected, interpreted or enacted? We should be aware of the groups to which the interviewee may give allegiance, or from which he or she draws his opinions. If there is a hidden audience whose later judgements have to be kept in mind we would do well to examine this explicitly with the interviewee.

Self-evaluation

Self-evaluation attracted ardent supporters during the 1980s. Workers such as Elliott (1980, 1981a, 1981b) and Hopkins (1985) stimulated experiments with it. Many others (for example, Holly, 1986a; Holly and Whitehead, 1986b) have taken it further, actively promoting the concept of the continuously evaluating and developing school. The GRIDS strategy (Guidelines for Review and Institutional Development in Schools, McMahon *et al*, 1984) offers a powerful tool for the cyclical approach to whole school development. Pastoral care cannot be separated from these movements without becoming fossilised. Valuable discussions can be found in Reid, Holly, and Hopkins (1987) and Wideen and Andrews (eds) (1987). My intent is to encourage pastoral heads to relate these initiatives to the pastoral sub-system, drawing attention to the perceptual and emotive processes which underlie attempts at self-evaluation. These approaches stress the teacher's skills of observation, the analysis of classroom interaction, and such tactics as shadowing pupils to gain awareness of the way the curriculum impinges on them. How many pastoral heads have set out to explore systematically the impact of tutor work and pastoral activities on the students? Forceful statements – positive, negative and indifferent – are made, but they often seem to be the product of prejudice or the unquestioned, immediate imposition of meaning. Evaluation of pastoral work can take place in at least four different ways:

- by the heads of year or house as a middle-management team;
- by the head of year or house with her or his team of tutors;
- between heads of academic departments and pastoral heads as part of the middle management of the school;
- as part of 'whole' school activity.

Pastoral heads might begin profitably by asking how pastoral activity helps the school achieve its educational objectives. A simple question, 'What does pastoral work contribute to the output of this school?' provokes thought. The answer to 'How would this school be different if pastoral activity was taken away?' might well cause shock. Reluctantly, my answer has sometimes been, 'Not much!'

The co-operation and conflicts between pastoral and academic heads merit far closer examination than they often receive. Alertness may show that superficial civility masks derogatory attitudes. Doherty (1977) found a tendency for departmental heads to see the head of year as a servant, dealing with tedious disciplinary problems or tiresome pupils. I have sometimes found resentment about the power seen as having accrued to the pastoral heads. Denial that these things exist, perpetuates stress and encourages Machiavellians who exploit tensions avidly, albeit that they cloak their activities in self-righteous or allegedly 'professional' justifications.

Much of the content of this book is relevant to self-evaluation of the pastoral head and her or his team of tutors. This is the arena in which misperceptions of the nature and purpose of pastoral work manifest themselves. It is tempting to avoid issues and build a shallow concord. If self-evaluation leads to training and support, the tensions are worthwhile. Fears of being 'turned into a social worker' operate; the implications of 'These kids know where they can get away with it, and they mustn't or the rot will spread' must be examined as barriers to progress.

Yet some conclude that self-evaluation has not lived up to expectations of it (for example, Clift *et al* (eds), 1987). The outcome may be complacency or confirmation that current practices are the only possible reaction to demands made in the contemporary climate. Closer inspection reveals a gamut of factors reducing the efficacy of self-evaluation. A major factor precipitating resistance and caution is accountability. Clift *et al* show that if self-evaluation leads to rendering an account of practice and standards to an outside group, the response is suspicion, and construction of a socially desirable façade.

Other forces erode the likelihood of changes being instituted as a response to self-evaluation. An obvious link with the Mannheimian thesis of social truth is present in the Clift *et al* volume. It is reported that in one school the meaning of the self-evaluation project *at each staff level* was 'renegotiated, redefined and appropriated by various groups and individuals' in service of their own purposes. Institutions have a remarkable capacity for damping down potential threat and obliterating change. The credibility of a self-evaluatory team is fragile in the eyes of other groups; negative intent is attributed to the originators of the project; and those who implement it attract hostility, especially if they are clumsy or manifestly insecure. Staff development has not learned that reactions to deep-seated anxiety are rarely straightforward. Senior management are scapegoated: occasionally their failure in communication and negotiation invites it. Poor communication interacts with anxiety to distort perceptions. Teachers are then apprehensive about the consequences of an activity which they see as disparaging and censuring rather than supportive. Threat is more intense for those in marginal positions in their sub-group, eg those who have good chances of promotion to a higher grade, or who have just gained it, but not established themselves. Yet, as Clift *et al* comment, self-evaluation involves young teachers who feel excluded from decision making. Two aspects of credibility therefore have to be considered: that of the activity; and, equally important, that of the pastoral head who initiates it.

Pastoral heads must acquire sound knowledge of judgemental and perceptual processes operating in work groups in school. Let me make it clear that this is not an incitement to arbitrary assessments, or messianic or revelatory pronouncements. A few year or house heads stupidly make immediate diagnoses which the experienced social or industrial psychologist would hesitate to endorse even when the evidence pointed towards them. Sound staff development stamps on such irrelevancies, but it is proper to recognise individual differences which shape work relationships. Rigidity and anxiety provide examples. Some of us tend to be tied to our original assessments of a situation or person, finding it difficult to relinquish them. Anxiety predisposes some individuals to have intense vigilant anticipations of threat which shape their reactions to any innovation. They then claim that it is 'dangerous', unprofessional or unethical. It is sensible to spend time deliberating about forms of presentation and explanation which will prevent such individuals adopting stances or taking resistive actions which cannot be abandoned without loss of face. Person perception researchers (for example Rommetweit, 1960; Jones *et al*, 1972 and Bem, 1972) provide salutary reminders of the subjectivity of person perception which pastoral heads should keep in mind. Rubenowitz (1968) produced evidence of pervasive tendencies towards rigidity or flexibility. As 'comprehensive dimensions of mind' they present a challenge which pastoral heads have to face. Cook (1979) provides an excellent overview which pastoral heads could use with profit. Person perception research reminds us how arbitrary our reactions are, especially when dissent to our proposals appears. It alerts us to the fact that although we honestly believe we are responding to a total situation, we are doing nothing of the kind. Identification of one salient characteristic, especially a threatening one, triggers off a sequence of automatic judgements which are rarely questioned. It is liberating to understand that beliefs and assumptions shape our perceptions more than we realise: perceptions then determine how we behave. Tackling the problem gives us a chance to escape from being a prisoner of our own point of view.

If self-evaluation is not to be barren, pastoral heads must be sensitive to the problems of perception which underlie colleagues' reactions to it. Prejudgement of motives, predictions about outcomes – or more cynically the lack of them – need to be understood and challenged if need be. Behaviour in evaluatory situations is complex: conflicting pressures towards co-operation and resistance are almost inevitable. Face-saving vies with honest concern for pupils. The labels attached to those initiating the self-evaluation assume greater significance than the process itself. It is imperative that pastoral heads study self-evaluation as an activity almost certainly marked by the presence of mixed motives.

An interesting introduction to the idea of mixed motives is given in *The Prisoner's Dilemma* by Luce and Raiffa (1957). The situation is:

Two suspects have been taken into custody where they are not allowed to communicate. The district attorney is certain that they both committed the serious crime with which they have been charged, but he does not have sufficient evidence to convict them at a trial. He explains to each prisoner that they have only two choices: to confess or not to confess. He states:

(i) That if both do not confess, they will both be booked on some minor charge and receive a sentence of one year.
(ii) If they both confess, they will be charged with the major crime, but he will recommend a lenient sentence of eight years.
(iii) If one confesses and the other does not, the confessor will receive a mild sentence of 3 months, while the other will get the full sentence of ten years.

He then leaves each one alone to decide whether he or she will confess or maintain that he or she is innocent.

The possibilities are outlined in the matrix below. The outcomes for each prisoner are indicated in each quadrant; those for Prisoner One coming first.

PRISONER TWO

	NOT CONFESS	CONFESS
NOT CONFESS	1 year; 1 year	10 years; 3 months
CONFESS	3 months; 10 years	8 years; 8 years

PRISONER ONE

Pressures towards mutual trust and co-operation are strong, but the temptation to betray and to be suspicious of each other is also strong.

Social psychologists have based powerful research on this problem (see for example Deutsch, 1974; Messick and Thorngate, 1967; and Rapaport and Chammah, 1965). Why? Because it reflects real-life circumstances containing mixed motives, especially competing tendencies towards co-operation and competition, trust and distrust, the hampering or facilitating of the task of the group. Unless brought into the open, mixed motives stultify attempts at self-evaluation.

Let us look at it from a different perspective. In 1974 I described the counselling interview as a market place in which an underlying process of bargaining and exchange is at work. If costs are too high, and the exchanges unrewarding or without meaning, counselling shrivels away. Self-appraisal seems to involve the same process in which honest appraisal is exchanged for acceptance and support. But is this the reality? The prospect of self-evaluation easily becomes contaminated with fear of loss of face. Participants feel cheated if they suspect that others are dissembling: the fairness and justice of the process is then questioned; withdrawal psychologically becomes the most attractive proposition. In negotiation, preservation of face is crucial. Those responsible for self-evaluation forget the vulnerability of colleagues. Even in industrial negotiation, seemingly trivial remarks or incidents unleash hostile or defensive reactions. The *self as a teacher* is challenged unhelpfully by inept attempts at self-evaluation. Personal concepts of weakness and inefficiency have been kept hidden from colleagues but self-evaluation may seem to threaten exposure. Empathy and caring are qualities that year heads should exemplify in their approach to self-evaluation.

Expectations may be given token recognition as an important element in success or failure of a self-evaluatory exercise but in practice they are often ignored. Group members' predictions about likely outcomes shape their interaction but it takes courage to challenge them. Feelings that inequity of effort is present, and the belief that contributions from certain members receive more favourable attention alter the input. An effective leader is alert to such feelings, but knows when to make concessions and when to be firm. The possibility of such difficulties has to be introduced in a neutral way as a necessary prelude to building a productive group.

It may be more common than one believes for groups to be plunged into alleged self-evaluation without anyone being clear about what they hope to accomplish. Then dissolution into incompetence and misunderstanding is almost inevitable.

Group dynamics have to be kept in mind. Affiliations and

antagonisms obviously need to be assessed, but there are hidden loyalties and suppressed oppositions which appear inconsequent, and therefore liable to misinterpretation. Projection of feelings and motives is fostered by the very nature of self-evaluation, especially in competitive individuals. Kelley and Stahleski (1970) for example, found that competitive individuals were likely to see others in the group as equally competitive, even if they were actually co-operative. The group leader needs to strive to create a climate of safety and mutual respect if self-evaluation is not to be swamped by the multiple and conflicting motives and feelings it arouses. Awareness is the major step in dealing with them.

To start the process a simple middle-management exercise is provided. As usual, adaptation will be needed.

Self-evaluation as a tool for staff development

---

1 A question for debate

In an earlier (1983) paper I raised the question, 'Is self-evaluation a tool or a trap?' In groups of six work on this question. Three members of the group take the standpoint that it is a trap, listing their reasons on a large sheet of paper. The other three take the positive viewpoint, similarly listing their reasons. After 15 minutes a group discussion occurs in which the point is explored by the six people.

---

2 Points to consider
A group of experienced teachers raised the following in their discussion. In your groups of six relate these apparently conflicting points to your earlier discussion.
    1 Trust increased through communication
    2 Threat introduced
    3 Risk of static labelling of teachers
    4 Production of more effective team work
    5 Innovation generated
    6 Business efficiency model
    7 Stimulus for further INSET

8 Perception of impossible demands for time and skill by classroom teacher

9 Attack on inert management stimulated

10 Organic model of school and development

11 Stimulation of a 'mass production' model of education

12 Establishment of clear criteria for evaluating efficiency

When you have finished your group discussion, work with a partner and ask what lies behind these different perceptions in a group with similar training and background.

3 The purposes of self-evaluation in pastoral work

3.1 If self-evaluation is used to blindly justify current procedures then it is a trap. If it helps heads of year or house, their tutors and others, explore the way pastoral activity helps the school achieve its educational objectives, and supports both pupils and teachers in the educational endeavour, it is potentially worthwhile. But it seems certain that self-evaluation intended to give a statement of accountability to some outside group will be perceived negatively, and arouse defensiveness. Negative intent and purpose is quickly ascribed to those promoting the scheme and suspicion and distrust manifest themselves. The credibility of the self-evaluation scheme then becomes low, perhaps non-existent.

3.2 Work in groups of six:
   (i) Decide what the objectives of a self-evaluation scheme for pastoral work should be.
   (ii) How would it operate? Try to specify:
   - what data you think would be needed;
   - what methods will be used, eg standard interviews, questionnaires, tutor group observation, problem identification;
   - how you would prevent it becoming unhelpfully judgemental.

3.3 Explain your plan with its underlying rationale to another group.

4 Does self-evaluation imply a total approach to the pastoral system?

4.1 Consider the possibility of self-evaluation of:
   (i) the heads of year or house as a team;
   (ii) individual heads of year or house with their teams of tutors.

4.2 In groups of six consider the arguments for and against self-evaluation of the heads of year or house as a team, eg
   (i) They may feel vulnerable and react badly to the suggestion.
   (ii) It could reinforce the sense of being a team.
   (iii) It may operate to reinforce established positions.

4.3 Then proceed to look at self-evaluation by a head of year and his/her team of tutors. What are the difficulties and rewards?

5 Taking a simple social systems approach in self-evaluation of pastoral work

5.1 Some simple ideas are set out below for you to build on:
   (i) Each school is a social system within which many forces interact, therefore direct comparability is difficult, if not delusory.
   (ii) Teachers should question their beliefs about the reasons for the problems faced by the school. Blind blame-pinning and labelling are all too common.
   (iii) A school holds apparently unrecognised contradictory and self-defeating behaviours. There are hidden agendas which may turn out to be as important as more obvious features of the school.

(iv) We may need to evaluate our relations with parents, the neighbourhood generally, and other professionals who have a legitimate concern with what happens within the school.

(v) We could ask why pupils lose their initial enthusiasm for pastoral work. What image of the teachers and the school build up unnoticed which influence reactions in later years?

(vi) What is inherent in our classroom interaction, control and disciplinary actions? Do they enhance or erode responsibility and self-control.

(vii) What predictions about the success or otherwise of certain pupils or groups are present in the educational organisation and our teaching methods?

(viii) Is the importance of achievement in the social and emotional areas given sufficient recognition?

5.2 Now in groups of four work out the content of a self-evaluation exercise which helps a head of year or house and his tutors take this wider approach. Share ideas with another group when your scheme has taken shape.

The points made in the paragraphs preceding the exercise could be met by treating self-evaluation as a group based problem-solving exercise. Fox (1987) offers in his Improved Nominal Group Technique a way of minimising the problems described earlier. Note that no attempt is made here to describe Fox's work: pastoral heads should read and adapt it themselves. Salient issues, however, are taken up. This valuable work is based on recognition of fears of rejection by the group, and the existence of hidden agendas about self-interest, or defending oneself against real or imagined threat. Group problem solving copes with the false perceptions of the problem held by individuals, and the unhelpful imposition of egocentric concerns. Status versus merit has to be tackled. The group leader's stranglehold on ideas – unwitting perhaps – has to be removed. Confusion between selling one's own ideas and building on the best ones has to be tackled. Pressure towards affiliation and the need for approval give the source of the idea precedence over its merit.

Fox usefully emphasises the need to limit and clarify the purposes of a problem-solving meeting. Clouding the issues by including too much undermines the problem-solving effort. Separate meetings are necessary for:

- identifying problems and establishing priorities;
- designing general plans for tackling the identified problems;
- resolving a particular problem.

The fact that status takes precedence over the quality of ideas may partially account for the reservations many teachers have about the effectiveness of self-evaluation. Fox is clear that those of either formal or informal lower status are reticent unless encouraged *and* protected from disparagement. Many good ideas are lost, and opportunities for involvement are reduced. Therefore anonymity of ideas is crucial. They can be written out on slips of paper and put into a ballot-type box in the staffroom so that they cannot be commented on in advance of the meeting. All suggestions are then transcribed on to large sheets of paper, and displayed throughout the meeting. Resistance to the temptation to rewrite or modify statements is an imperative. Participants come to the meeting with something to say – positive or negative – that is considered. All displayed ideas are discussed before decisions are made. Assurance that one's ideas will be considered further increases the probability of involvement. Keeping to target is prime: one of Fox's principles is that discussion in such meetings should be confined to essential clarification, and the advantages or disadvantages of specific ideas. Vigilance is necessary if small group work is included. I find teachers, even when given structured material, have a strong propensity to deviate into somewhat self-indulgent anecdotal interaction, evading the tasks. Humorous intervention at the *first* signs of this seems to work.

The anonymous pre-meeting activities can include answers to the question, 'What risks or difficulties do you believe exist in the proposed self-evaluation programme?' Broad understanding of colleagues' attitudes and orientations can be garnered from anonymous replies to some appropriate version of 'What would you most like to see the school doing in five years' time, and least like to see it doing in five years' time?' Responses could be displayed anonymously and discussed at a preliminary meeting.

Two points. I have found the idea of establishing priorities by selecting the most important item and the least important item, and then choosing the second most important and the second least important item helpful. The group proceeds in this manner until all the possibilities have been examined. Next, the wise leader preserves the data from the flipcharts in an orderly and readily retrievable way for use in future sessions.

Staff appraisal

Pastoral heads are probably no longer characters in search of a role, but they must keep their roles flexible. Staff appraisal or review and development, as described by the Somerset Project Team (1988), will extend their sphere of professional activity. Used sensitively, staff appraisal could be a powerful tool for individual and institutional development. It is also fraught with tensions, and liable to unexpected drawbacks, to which pastoral heads should apply their skills in social–emotional leadership and counselling. Innovations fail when problems are not anticipated, and unintended consequences manifest themselves. Feelings shape behaviours: strong emotions have been aroused by appraisal and year or house heads must explore the irrationalities with their tutors. This section, therefore, is not intended as an overview of review and development. It concentrates on associated feelings and subjective elements and skills which are at the heart of pastoral work. What was said about interviewing and self-evaluation is equally germane to review and development.

Be clear that it is a *process* rather than an annual event. The Somerset Project is clear that carefully structured follow-up INSET is an integral part of review and development, essential for its credibility. Four elements have to be examined: the methods employed; the appraised; the appraiser; and the school context in which the review occurs. Failure to take any one, or combination, of them into account invites distorted understandings and abortive actions. It is unrealistic to ignore the complications aroused by the highly emotive climate in which the original conception was formulated. Teachers have claimed it is an indirect technique of control, used to keep them in line through imposing constraining norms. Others feared that it could be a precursor to dispensing with teachers who oppose senior management's arbitrary policies. Here the position taken is that it is an activity potentially of great benefit to both teachers and students, although in the long-run prone to distortion and ineffectiveness.

If we approach review and development positively, as I believe we should, we do not have to be unrealistic. Staff appraisal is not inevitably tied to career advancement. Teaching currently is a contracting industry; anxiety about reduced promotion opportunities is cited as a source of stress. Appraisal is about increasing teachers' job satisfaction, and reinforcing in precise ways their sense of efficacy, ie of being in positive control of their professional life. *It must be a tool for maintaining and increasing positive mental health* as outlined earlier. Let us see it as formative assessment for the teacher. In formative assessment we work *with* the students, analysing their strengths and weaknesses, encouraging them to identify their own contributions to indifferent performance, pinpointing areas of competence which can be built on, setting realistic but stretching targets, working out methodically the steps that have to be taken to achieve them. No more and no less is required of the teacher. Both have to perceive the ways in which they defeat themselves.

What difficulties arise for the head of house or year as an appraiser? Probably the initial hurdle will be whole-hearted acceptance of their role as appraiser. They may feel that it will destroy their relationships with tutors. At the lowest level, the rejoinder must be, 'Are these relationships so positive now?' If I have read the evidence aright, the process of appraisal, if well done, facilitates formation of purposeful, task-orientated relationships. Failure to recognise inconsistencies between what is said and what is done again distort interaction. Pastoral heads sincerely voice their regrets about tutors' inadequacy and lack of commitment to pastoral work. Yet paradoxically, the very same people are reluctant to face the implications of the fact that they are the tutors' immediate superiors. The failure to do so makes them a drag on the system and a brake on progress. As a middle-management team they must ask, 'Is the head of year or house to be held responsible for the performance of an inadequate tutor?' The ramifications of this question are great, possibly taking them back to team failure to educate colleagues about the purposes and methods of pastoral care. The conclusions can be compared with the responsibilities of a departmental head for one of his subject team. Submerged tensions will fester until such ambiguities are removed.

Preparatory team work for their appraiser roles must include investigation of styles of judgement which influence many situations. (The neglect of this found in some INSET work on profiling is disturbing.) Some might become aware of a marked tendency towards undue generosity in their judgements – the personality dynamics or underlying motives are not so important as detecting and modifying the tendency. Significant differences between individuals are obscured through massive and unjustified – possibly unjustifiable – 'giving the tutor the benefit of the doubt'. Such apparent kindness may actually condemn the young tutor to continued incompetence and give the older ones a licence to continue in complacent rejection of the tutor role. Others might inject their 'weary' cynicism into the appraisal. As in general social interaction, selective perception will be at work: as we assume, so do we perceive. Some behaviours will be highlighted consistently; others will have their significance ignored. Appraisers must be aware of their idiosyncratic assumptions. Vulnerability to the well-known 'halo' effect brings danger of reliance on a general impression which then ignores variations in specific skills and attitudes. Even when criteria are laid down, in practice they are subject to interpretation by the appraiser. What is a good standard of achievement for one person is mediocre for another. Although the appraised will take responsibility for setting their own targets and working out the steps to be taken, it would be naïve to deny that such factors are at work.

Proper stress should be given to classroom observation but a critical stance has to be maintained. Essential questions are:

1 How representative is the sample of observations of the observed's total range of behaviours relevant to the appraisal? Is it valid to generalise from them, even if they are accurate?
2 How aware is the observer of any selectivity in his or her observations? Is he or she relying on crude, unchecked formulae about effective classroom interaction and implicit notions of the 'good' teacher?
3 Has sufficient allowance been made for variations between classes, the impact of time of day or day of the week, current mental and physical conditions of observer and observed, and the effect of being observed?

The message: a proper humility about the reliability and validity of our observations – even if rapport exists between observed and observer – constrains incautious generalisations and marks the beginning of wisdom.

As both appraised and appraiser, pastoral heads should be aware that honesty is not necessarily accuracy. Reactions are genuine, yet unknowingly they are shaped by extraneous factors. Group affiliations and the Mannheimian view of the truth are obvious examples.

Idiosyncratic interpretations of the nature of teaching, and the tasks legitimately part of it, trigger off misunderstandings.

The value climate or culture of the school will have a pervasive influence on appraisal. Expectations gain legitimacy, ie the sense of rightness, and because appraisal is carried out by members of a school within the context of that school, they operate to shape the appraisal without being evaluated themselves. Goffman's work (1961; 1971) illuminates such processes. These remarks brought to me memories of the old work on a mental hospital infiltrated by doctors posing as patients. They behaved rationally but this was interpreted by staff as 'resistance to treatment' or 'defensive refusal to face reality'. It was not until they met the expectations of the staff about the illness diagnosed in their invented case histories, and worked through the stages deemed essential for 'cure', that they were discharged. (My intent is not to discuss the reality of the stages but to show the compulsive hold of expectations.) A chill strikes me when I ponder on the likelihood that an initially constructive process of review and development could, after a few years, incorporate similar unthinking practices.

When the culture of the school is permeated by distrust, anxiety or suspicion, appraisal will not be immune to them. Teachers' fears are not inevitably unrealistic: the old gag, 'Because you're paranoid, it doesn't mean that they're not out to get you!', can be disconcertingly apt. Review and development coinciding with a major disjunction or period of threat for the school takes on new dimensions. The prospect of closure or amalgamation inevitably colours perceptions of the motives of the appraiser and the intent of the review. Complications ensue when an autocratic head who fostered dependency in his or her staff retires, and a democratic one follows. Some cling to their desire to be directed: for a larger percentage the legacy of the past produces distrust of the new incumbent; the belief is that suddenly he or she will pounce, revealing what lies behind the mask. Introduction of review in such an atmosphere may lead to passive resistance or the attempt to produce what the teacher believes the head wants. A school dominated by dependence on a charismatic head is anti-pathetic to the challenge and enterprise of review and development. Reliance on routines inculcated by mechanistic forms of management again accords ill with the initiative and purposeful striving which should be the outcome of the review.

Vigilance has to be maintained lest emergent and/or unanticip-ated events reduce the efficiency of appraisal schemes. If the credibility of the appraisers and the outcomes of the reviews are insufficiently monitored, then the 'group think' of the sub-populations commented on in Chapter One will be marked by increasing cynicism. Co-operation is then withdrawn: its appearance may be there, but individuals, almost unknown to themselves, conspire to turn the process into a charade. The importance and benefits of review and development are lost, denying the fact that it is a civilised activity producing constructive professional interdependence – a new expression of Durkheim's (1933) organic solidarity. In terms of professional pride, development and independence I welcome it as part of re-establishing the school as a significant community in relation to the larger society. But poor appraisal conducted in a negative spirit would strengthen tutelage, professional dependency and conflict rather than mutuality.

Review will be an uneasy, even distasteful, experience for the teacher whose professional life is dominated by adherence to simple formulae about discipline and interaction. Those over-sensitive to the norms of their staff sub-group will be alert to the hidden audience whose later judgements act as sanctions. They have false expectations, assuming that review means immediate clarity and precision. Uncertainty and challenge make them bluster or retreat anxiously. We have to guard against invidious comparison entering the review and insidiously undermining it. The appraised is as likely to introduce it as the appraiser. Radloff (1968) shows that the need for self-evaluation prompts comparison of oneself with others. Clumsy appraisal will stimulate defensive comparisons. Heads of year or house have, as part of their contribution to review and development, to take seriously the possibility that unintended aberrations can subvert it.

The possibility of fusing counselling principles with appraisal is well demonstrated by the Somerset work. We must also accept that power and appraisal, despite the latter being conducted sensitively, are intrinsically linked. Pastoral heads, as people with an especial concern for the care of colleagues, have to be especially watchful for the first signs of Machiavellianism entering appraisal. A Machiavellian uses power in human relationships for her or his own ends. A crucial distinction has to be made between the *orientation* to do this, and *skill* in doing it without detection. This explains the need for vigilance: the Machiavellian who is skilful strives to keep his or her machinations below the level of visibility. Skill is needed to detect these cool, calculating managers of impressions who take a grossly utilitarian view of their interaction with others. Payoffs are their focus rather than the well-being of others. They cloak self-advantage by a façade of concern.

Christie and Geis (1970) argue that Machiavellians are especially active in environments characterised by rapid change and ambiguity. My observations suggest that value conflicts and the current sense of devaluation in the profession provide grist for the Machiavellian's mill. Machiavellians as described in the research dismiss self-exploration as twaddle – unless it is expedient not to – they have little perceived need for personal change, and focus on status and reward.

Machiavellians will not be disturbed by appraisal: they will use it. They are always prepared to violate their private opinions by their behaviours if this is profitable. They take initiatives because, in their world of move versus counter-move, they believe this gives them the advantage. Attempts to change them fail because they have developed resistance to social influence: their strategems have to be exposed, and the payoff denied them.

My aim has been preventive. In a turbulent situation of largely unpredictable change there is the possibility that a worthwhile enterprise – review and development – could unwittingly cause Machiavellianism to have enlarged importance in secondary schools. Anticipation of possibilities is part of contingency planning. Yet it can be problematical. Clumsy actions may provoke the situation one hopes to avoid. If anticipation of difficulties is successful, then we may question its necessity. A final point: review and development is at its best when it embodies Tyler's (1969) principle of extending the good that exists; to me, that is at the heart of staff development, and its main justification.

Discussion activities follow which have been used to help pastoral heads clarify their ideas, and develop a co-operative approach. As with any new intervention we should debate the issues vigorously, including matters of ethics.

NB Each section in the exercise demands that at least one session be spent on it.

Staff appraisal: initial discussion activities

1 The intent of the activity

1.1 To help course participants examine key questions in an open-minded way.

1.2 To show the complexity of the appraisal process.

1.3 To stimulate awareness of the subjectivity and ambiguities of attempts at appraisal.

1.4 To show the potential benefits of a well-designed and professional scheme of appraisal.

2 A basic question: Is it possible to appraise teachers validly?

2.1 Byrne (1987) argues that we lack methods of appraisal which are intellectually sound, reasonably valid and feasible. He argues that appraisers have to resort to reliance upon inferences which allow 'considerable latitude in <u>what</u> is observed and <u>how</u> to interpret observations.' (Underlining not in the original.)

2.2 The categories used in appraisal tend to be vague and are not related closely enough to the situation. Byrne points out that teachers perform effectively in some situations, and not in others. Pupils also vary, therefore this needs to be taken into account. Are such situational differences taken sufficiently into account?

2.3 The teacher may be unreliable as a source of information or explanation. He or she may be honest but mistaken: they see the situation or behaviour from an idiosyncratic perspective.

2.4 Noting a poor performance does not explain its causes; it does not say whether it is due to lack of competence, the particular situation or some combination of the two.

2.5 The intent of the teacher may be taken for granted by the observer who fails to check the accuracy of his assumptions.

2.6 *Discussion tasks*

    (i) Appraise the relevance of these cautions about teacher appraisal. How would you allow for them?

    (ii) Make your own list of difficulties raised by teacher appraisal. Group them under the headings of:

        A *Methods*   B *Perceptual and attitudinal* (An example is distrust of the appraiser.)

Explain *and* justify your analysis to the group members.

---

3 Appraisal for what purposes?

3.1 The HMI Study (1985) distinguishes between:
- *evaluation* which is a general term describing any activity where the quality of provision is sytematically studied;
- *review* which is seen as retrospective study involving collection and examination of the evidence;
- *appraisal* where the emphasis is on forming a qualitative judgement;
- *assessment* which is a form of measurement or grading based on known criteria.

Discuss these useful distinctions. Note the significance of 'qualitative' in the definition of appraisal.

3.2 Appraisal can have sinister connotations in the minds of teachers. Reynolds (1987) argues that opposition to appraisal is based on the belief that it is politically rather than educationally inspired. There seem to be a number of reasons for appraisal which should be considered carefully:

    (i) It is a mechanism for identifying and dismissing inadequate teachers.

  (ii) It is concerned with career development, providing evidence of suitability for promotion.

 (iii) Marland (1987) sees appraisal as encouraging the teacher and building on good practice. Appraisal is therefore seen as a formative process in which the teacher's standard of performance is developed.

 (iv) Warwick (1983) sees appraisal as set within a managerial structure in which levels of responsibility are clearly defined. Regular meetings occur between 'each member of staff and his direct superior to assess progress and set targets for future development.' The staff member is to be given help in overcoming his weaknesses, and assisted in achieving his ambitions.

  (v) Dadds (1987) argues that appraisal should be related to the long-run purposes of the school, and involve a sense of purposeful control over the process as a prerequisite for learning from it.

 (vi) Marland (see (iii) above) cites Smyth (1985) who sees appraisal as an 'emancipatory or liberating process through which teachers assist each other to gain control over their own professional lives and destinies.'

3.3 Consider the views above. Now work out in your group:
  – what staff appraisal *ought* to be about;
  – what it will *probably* be about.
If you felt the reality of appraisal might be negative what could be done to prevent this happening?

---

4 The appraisers

4.1 Who should be charged with the task of appraisal? Who should appraise the head? To whom will the results of appraisal be known?

4.2 What stresses do the appraisers face? HMI Study (1985) reports that none of the schools surveyed

gave training in appraisal or interview techniques.
Training in classroom observation skills may also
be necessary.

4.3 The skills of counselling are needed. Diffey (1987)
draws attention to:

 (i) The need to let the appraisee make his/her
points in his/her own words.

 (ii) Use the skill of clarification through reflective
and supportive questions.

 (iii) Respond to feelings.

 (iv) Listen rather than talk.

 (v) Try to use the appraisee's frame of reference.

 (vi) Be prepared to modify perceptions in the light
of later information rather than close early and
refuse to admit further evidence.

4.4 An analytic and problem-solving approach is
essential, in which the appraiser helps the other
think about the problem in ways which suggest the
steps that can be taken to deal with it.

4.5 The appraiser must give the appraised the sense of
'owning' the appraisal so that she/he is involved in
it. Without this, responsibility is renounced, and the
appraised retreats to 'tell me what to do!'

4.6 Appraisers may feel great anxiety about their
adequacy for the role. Fear of causing harm makes
them retreat: honesty may be confused with
destructive confrontation; this then makes the
process innocuous but anti-developmental. No
learning occurs and nothing changes.

4.7 Discuss the approaches to teacher appraisal set
out above. Now make your own statements about
the *skills* and *attitudes* needed by appraisers. Be
as precise as possible. Comment on the in-service
training that will be needed.

5 The process of appraisal

5.1 Initial self-appraisal seems essential if appraisees
are to feel active participants in the process. Turner

(1987) suggests useful themes that could be part of the self-appraisal. (I have modified them slightly.)

   (i) Use of time, including the balance of 'busy work' versus meaningful work. The time allocated to educational thinking, and the tendency towards passive reaction or active mastery needs thought.

   (ii) Responsibilities and their relationships to one another. Appraisal is not to be confined to teaching and classroom interaction.

   (iii) Jobs can be interpreted very differently; the expectations of others shape performance; enactment is influenced by the context operating in the school.

The appraisee who has thought open-mindedly about the above is likely to make fuller use of the appraisal experience.

5.2 Discuss, and then prepare recommendations for, effective preparation for the first appraisal interview by both appraisee and appraisers.

5.3 The appraisal interview could be seen usefully as a guidance interview in which the appraised constructs a plan for development and the appraiser identifies sources of difficulty, barriers and routes to the desired goal. Material from structured self-observation and analysis by the appraisee can be used; the results of 'shadowing' or classroom/tutorial period observations are included. Note that this is not based on some global concept of 'the effective teacher' but on how the individual teacher's job satisfaction and com-petence can be increased in the circumstances in which she/he works. Ideally, appraisal is about constructing an agreed strategy for development. *Discuss the view given above* which is supportive and rewarding of areas of strength.

5.4 Note that it is very common for the secondary school teacher to hide or disguise his or her problems because they feel others will label or condemn them. How will this impinge on the appraisal interview?

5.5 Follow-up is essential. Targets have to be agreed, methods of change discussed, supports provided and periodic consultations arranged. The timing has to be adapted to the workloads of those concerned. Seasonal pressures on teachers have to be taken into account. Without a step-by-step approach, and the opportunity for consultation, the effort invested will be wasted.

Discuss your ideas of adequate and contructive follow-up. The following questions are worthy of thought:

(i) How does one maintain as both appraised and appraiser a healthy balance between professional autonomy and adaptation to the needs of the school?

(ii) What precautions have to be taken to prevent appraisal becoming a subtle form of coercion or eroding initiative?

6 Ethics

6.1 Profiles are regarded properly as the property of the pupil who decides what use is to be made of them. A formative process is at work in teacher appraisal, but whose property is the record of it? Jenks (1987) argues that current performance, not past performance, is what matters. The problem of confidentiality cannot be dismissed lightly. A system where the ethical issues are ignored deserves to be distrusted.

6.2 In a profession the appraiser must also be appraised. This includes the head. How much confidence will staff have in outside appraisers of the head?

6.3 If appraisals are seen to be related to promotion, then there is the danger that this could distort the appraisal process, and erode openness and honesty.

6.4 The desire for harmony may become an end in itself; the appraisal documents and the exercise itself may evade issues and maintain a comfortable but unproductive state of affairs.

6.5 If the appraiser is known to be incompetent or untrustworthy has the appraised the right to ask for another person to undertake the appraisal?

6.6 Discuss these points, adding any other ethical questions which come to mind.

References

Adair, J. (1986) *Effective Team Leadership*, Aldershot: Gower.

Ames, C. and Ames, R. (Eds.) (1984) *Research on Motivation in Education*, London: Academic Press.

Anderson, H. and Brewer, J. (1946) *Studies of Teachers' Classroom Personalities, I. Dominative and Socially Integrative Behaviour of Kindergarten Teachers*. No. 6. Applied Psychology Monographs.

Anderson, H. and Brewer, J. (1946) *Studies of Teachers' Classroom Personalities, II. Effects of Teachers' Dominative and Integrative Contacts on Children's Classroom Behaviours*. No. 8. Applied Psychology Monographs.

Anderson, H., Brewer, J. and Reed, M. (1946) *Studies of Teachers' Classroom Personalities, III. Follow-up Studies of the Effects of Dominative and Integrative Contacts on Children's Behaviour*. No. 11. Applied Psychology Monographs.

Ansoff, H. (1984) *Implanting Strategic Management*, Englewood Cliffs, N.J.: Prentice Hall.

Argyis, C., Putnam, R. and Smith, D. (1985) *Action Science*, San Francisco: Jossey-Bass.

Argyis, C. and Schon, D. (1974) *Theory Into Practice: Increasing Professional Effectiveness*, San Francisco: Jossey-Bass.

Aronfreed, J. (1968) *Conduct and Conscience: The Socialization of Internalized Control Over Behavior*, New York: Academic Press.

Ausubel, D. (1968) *Eductional Psychology: A Cognitive View*, New York: Holt, Rinehart and Winston.

Bales, R. (1970) *Personality and Interpersonal Behavior*, New York: Holt, Rinehart and Winston.

Ballinger, E. (1984) *Management Development Outside Education: Some Implications for the NDC*, Bristol: National Development Centre for School Management Training.

Banaka, W. (1971) *Training in Depth Interviewing* (later editions available), New York: Harper.

Bandura, A. (1986) 'The Explanatory and Predictive Scope of Self-Efficacy Theory', *Journal of Social and Clinical Psychology*, 41, pp 586–598.

Bellack, A. (1963) (Ed.) *Theory and Research in Teaching*, New York: Teachers College, Columbia University.

Bellack, A., Kliebard, H., Hyman, R. and Smith, F. (1966) *The Language of the Classroom*, New York: Teachers College, Columbia University.

Bem, D. (1972) 'Self-Perception Theory', in Berkowitz, L. (Ed.) *Advances in Experimental Social Psychology*, New York: Academic Press.

Bennett, N. and Desforges, C. (Eds.) (1985) *Recent Advances in Classroom Research*, Edinburgh: Scottish Academic Press.

Bennett, S. (1974) *The School: An Organizational Analysis*, Glasgow: Blackie.

Berne, E. (1964) *Games People Play*, London: Deutsch.

Bion, W. (1961) *Experience in Groups*, London: Tavistock.

Bradford, D. and Cohen, A. (1984) *Managing for Excellence*, New York: Wiley.

Bradley, J., Chesson, R. and Silverleaf, J. (1983) *Inside Staff Development*, Windsor: NFER.

Brehm, J. and Cohen, A. (1962) *Explorations in Cognitive Dissonance*, New York: Wiley.

Brophy, J. and Good, T. (1974) *Teacher–Student Relationships*, New York: Holt, Rinehart and Winston.

Brophy, J. and Good, T. (1979) *Teacher–Student Relationships*, 2nd Edition, New York: Holt, Rinehart and Winston.

Bruner, J. (1966) *Towards a Theory of Instruction*, Cambridge, Mass.: Harvard University Press.

Bruner, J. and Taguiri, R. (1954) 'The Perception of People', in Lindsey, G. (Ed.) *Handbook of Social Psychology*, Cambridge, Mass.: Addison-Wesley.

Buckley, J. (1980) 'The Care of Learning: Some Implications for School Organisation', in Best, R. *et al* *Perspectives in Pastoral Care*, London: Heinemann.

Buckley, J. (1985) *The Training of Secondary Heads in Western Europe*, Windsor: NFER.

Bunnell, S. (1987) (Ed.) *Teacher Appraisal in Practice*, London: Heinemann.

Burns, R. (1982) *Self-Concept Development and Education*, London: Holt, Rinehart and Winston.

Bush, T. (1986) *Theories of Educational Management*, London: Harper.

Buss, A. (1980) *Self-Consciousness and Anxiety*, San Francisco: Freeman.

Byrne, C. (1987) 'Can Teachers be Validly Appraised?', in Bunnell, S. (Ed.) *Teacher Appraisal in Practice*, London: Heinemann.

Calderhead, J. (1984) *Teachers' Classroom Decision-Making*, London: Holt, Rinehart and Winston.

Carpenter, S. and Kennedy, W. (1988) *A Practical Guide to Handling Conflict and Reaching Agreements*, San Francisco: Jossey-Bass.

Christie, R. and Geis, F. (1970) *Studies in Machiavellianism*, New York: Academic Press.

Clift, P., Nuttall, D. and McCormick, R. (1987) (Eds.) *Studies in School Self-Evaluation*, Lewes: Falmer.

Cohen, L. and Cohen, A. (1987) *Disruptive Behaviour*, London: Harper.

Cook, M. (1979) *Perceiving Others*, London: Methuen.

Coopersmith, S. (1967) *The Antecedents of Self-Esteem*, San Francisco: Freeman.

Coser, L. (1965) *The Functions of Social Conflict*, London: Routledge and Kegan Paul.

Coulby, D. and Harper, T. (1985) *Preventing Classroom Disruption*, London: Croom Helm.

Covington, M. and Beery, R. (1976) *Self-Worth and School Learning*, New York: Holt, Rinehart and Winston.

Cuban, L. (1984) 'Transforming the Frog into a Prince: Effective Schools Research, Policy and Practice at the District Level', *Harvard Educational Review*, Vol. 34, pp. 129–151.

Dadds, M. (1987) 'Learning and Teaching Appraisal: the Heart of the Matter', *School Organization*. Vol. 7. No. 2.

Dansereau, D. (1988) 'Co-operative learning strategies', in Weinstein, C. *et al* (Eds.) *Learning and Study Strategies*, New York: Academic Press.

D'Arienzo, R., Moracco, J. and Krajewski, R. (1982) *Stress in Teaching*, Washington: University Press of Nebraska.

Davies, I. (1976) *Objectives in Curriculum Design*, London: McGraw-Hill.

Dawson, R. (1982) 'Non-Attendance: The Barnsley Approach', *Association of Educational Psychologists Journal*, Vol. 5. No. 10, pp. 50–51.

De Charms, R. (1968) *Personal Causation*, New York: Academic Press.

Deci, E. and Ryan, R. (1985) *Intrinsic Motivation and Self-Determination in Human Behaviour*, New York: Plenum.

DES (1988) *Careers Education and Guidance from 5 to 16*, Curriculum Matters 10, London: HMSO.

Deutsch, M. (1973) *The Resolution of Conflict*, London: Yale University Press.

Diffey, K. (1987) 'How to Conduct a Teacher Appraisal Interview', *School Organization*, Vol. 7. No. 2.

Dobson, C. (1982) *Stress*, Lancaster: MTP Press.

Doherty, K. (1977) 'An Evaluation of a Pastoral Care System of a Comprehensive School in South Wales', Unpublished M.Ed. Dissertation, University College of Swansea.

Doherty, K. (1981) 'A Framework for the Evaluation of Pastoral Care', in Hamblin, D. (Ed.) *Problems and Practice of Pastoral Care*, Oxford: Blackwell.

Doyle, W. (1983) 'Academic Work', *Review of Educational Research*, Vol. 53. No. 2, pp. 159–199.

Dunham, J. (1984) *Stress in Teaching*, London: Croom Helm.

Durkheim, E. (1933) *The Division of Labour in Society*, New York: Collier-Macmillan.

Egglestone, J. (Ed.) (1979) *Teacher Decision-Making in The Classroom*, London: Routledge and Kegan Paul.

Elkind, D. (1970) *Children and Adolescents*, New York: Oxford University Press.

Eliot, T. S. (1949) *The Cocktail Party*, London: Faber and Faber.

Eliot, T. S. (1957) *On Poetry and Poets*, London: Faber and Faber.

Elliot, J. (1980) 'Implications of Classroom Research for Professional Development', in Hoyle, E. and Megarry, J. (Eds.) *World Yearbook 1980*, London: Kogan Page.

Elliot, J. (1981(a)) 'The Teacher as Researcher Within Award-Bearing Courses', in Alexander, R. and Ellis, J. (Eds.) *Advanced Study for Teachers*, Society for Research Into Higher Education, London: Nafferton.

Elliot, J. (1981(b)) *Action-Research: A Framework for Self-Evaluation in Schools*, Cambridge: CIE/Schools Council TIQL Project Working Paper.

Endler, N., Hunt, J. and Rosenstein, A. (1962) *An S–R Inventory of Anxiousness*, Psychological Monographs, Vol. 7. No. 17. Whole No. 536.

Festinger, L. (1957) *A Theory of Cognitive Dissonance*, Evanston, Ill: Row, Peterson.

Fox, W. *Effective Group Problem-Solving*, San Francisco: Jossey-Bass.

Frieze, I. *et al* (1983) 'Defining Success in Classroom Settings', in Levine, J. and Wang, C. (Eds.) *Teacher and Student Perceptions: Implications for Learning*, Hillsdale, N.J.: Erlbaum Associates.

Fullan, M. (1982) *The Meaning of Educational Change*, New York: Teachers College, Columbia University.

Fullan, M. (1986) 'Improving the Implementation of Educational Change', *School Organization*, Vol. 3.

Fullan, M., Miles, M. and Taylor, G. (1980) 'Organization Development in Schools: The State of the Art', *Review of Educational Research*, Vol. 50, 1, pp. 121–183.

Fullan, M., Miles, M. and Taylor, G. Cited in Schmuck, R. and Runkel, P. (1985) (3rd Edn.) *The Handbook of Organization Development in Schools*, Palo Alto: Mayfield Publishing Co.

Gibson, Q. (1960) *The Logic of Social Enquiry*, London: Routledge and Kegan Paul.

Goffman, E. (1959) *The Presentation of Self in Everyday Life*, New York: Doubleday.

Goffman, E. (1967) *Interaction Ritual*, London: Allen Lane.

Goffman, E. (1971) *Relations in Public*, London: Allen Lane.

Goodman, N. (1984) *On Mind and Other Matters*, Cambridge, Mass: Harvard University Press.

Griffin, G. (Ed.) (1983) *National Society for the Study of Education Yearbook Eightytwo: Part 2. Staff Development*, Chicago: University of Chicago Press.

Gross, N., Giacquinta, J. and Bernstein, M. (1971) *Implementing Organizational Innovations*, New York: Harper.

Hamblin, D. (1974) *The Teacher and Counselling*, Oxford: Blackwell.

Hamblin, D. (1977) 'The Pastoral Team: Illusion or Reality', *Journal of National Association of Careers and Guidance Teachers*. Summer.

Hamblin, D. (1978) *The Teacher and Pastoral Care*, Oxford: Blackwell.

Hamblin, D. (1981) *Teaching Study Skills*, Oxford: Blackwell.

Hamblin, D. (1984) *Pastoral Care: a Training Manual*, Oxford: Blackwell.

Hamblin, D. (1986) *A Pastoral Programme*, Oxford: Blackwell.

Handy, C. and Aitken, R. (1986) *Understanding Schools as Organisations*, Harmondsworth: Penguin.

Hare, W. (1985) *Controversies in Teaching*, London, Ontario: Althouse Press.

Hargreaves, A. (1979) 'Strategies, Decisions and Control in a Middle School Classroom', in Egglestone, J. (Ed.) *Teacher Decision-Making in the Classroom*, London: Routledge and Kegan Paul.

Hargreaves, D. (1967) *Social Relations in a Secondary School*, London: Routledge and Kegan Paul.

Hargreaves, D. (1982) *The Challenge for the Comprehensive School*, London: Routledge and Kegan Paul.

Heider, F. (1958) *The Psychology of Interpersonal Relations*, New York: Wiley.

Hersey, P. and Blanchard, K. (1977) *Management of Organizational Behavior: Utilizing Human Resources* (3rd Edn.) Englewood Cliffs, NJ: Prentice Hall.

Himes, J. (1980) *Conflict and Conflict Management*, Athens: University of Georgia Press.

Hitchcock, G. (1988) *Education and Training 14–18: A Survey of New Initiatives*, London: Longman.

HMI Study (1985) *Quality in Schools: Evaluation and Appraisal*, London: HMSO.

Holly, P. (1986) *The Teachers' Guide*, CIE/TRIST Working Paper, Cambridge Institute of Education.

Holly, P. and Whitehead, D. (Eds.) (1984) *Action Research in Schools: Getting It Into Perspective*: Bulletin No. 6. CARN Publications, Cambridge Institute of Education.

Holly, P. and Whitehead, D. (Eds.) (1986) *Collaborative Action Research*, Bulletin No. 7. CARN Publications, Cambridge Institute of Education.

Howard, A., Nance, D. and Myers, P. (1987) *Adaptive Counselling and Therapy*, San Francisco: Jossey-Bass.

Ivey, A. (1986) *Developmental Therapy*, San Francisco: Jossey-Bass.

Jenks, O. (1987) in Bunnell, S. (Ed.) (See above).

Jones, A. (1980) 'The School's View of Non-Attendance', in Hersov, L. and Berg, I. (Eds.) *Out of School*, Chichester: Wiley.

Jones, A. (1987) *Leadership for Tomorrow's Schools*, Oxford: Blackwell.

Jones, E. and Nisbett, R. (1972) 'The Actor and the Observer: Divergent Perceptions of the Causes of Behavior', in Jones, E. *et al.* (See below.)

Jones, E., Kanouse, D., Kelley, H., Nisbett, R., Valins, S. and Weiner, B. (Eds.) *Attribution: Perceiving the Causes of Behaviour*, Morriston, NJ: General Learning Press.

Joyce, B., Hersch, R. and McKibbin, M. (1983) *The Structure of School Improvement*, New York: Longman.

Kanfer, F. and Goldstein, A. (Eds.) (1985) *Helping People Change* (3rd Edn.), New York: Pergamon.

Kay, W. (1968) *Moral Development and Behaviour*, London: Allen and Unwin.

Kelley, H. and Stahleski, A. (1970) 'Social Interaction Basis of Co-operator's and Competitor's Beliefs About Others', *Journal of Personality and Social Psychology*, Vol. 16, No. 1, pp. 61–91..

Kelman, H. (1958) 'Compliance, Identification and Internalization: Three Processes of Attitude Change', *Journal of Conflict Resolution*, 2, pp. 51–60.

King, C. (1984) 'The Secondary Head as Leader', in Harling, P. (Ed.) *New Directions in Educational Leadership*, London: Falmer.

King, R. (1973) *School Organization and Pupil Involvement*, London: Routledge and Kegan Paul.

Knutton, S. and Mycroft, A. (1986) 'Stress and the Deputy Head', *School Organization*, Vol. 6. No. 1.

Kohlberg, L. (1976) 'Moral Stages and Moralization: The Cognitive-Developmental Approach', in Lickona, T. (Ed.) *Moral Development and Behavior*, New York: Holt, Rinehart and Winston.

Kolb, D. (1983) *The Mediators*, Cambridge, Mass: MIT Press.

Kolb, D. (1984) *Experiential Learning*, Englewood Cliffs, NJ: Prentice Hall.

Kolvin, I., Garside, N., Nicol, A., Macmillan, F., Wolstenholme, I. and Leitch, I. (1986) *Help Starts Here: The Maladjusted Child in the Ordinary School*, London: Tavistock-Methuen.

Krumboltz, J. and Thoresen, C. (1969) *Behavioral Counseling*, New York: Holt, Rinehart and Winston.

Kyriacou, C. (1986) *Effective Teaching in Schools*, Oxford: Blackwell.

Kyriacou, C. and Sutcliffe, J. (1978) 'Teacher Stress: Prevalence, Sources and Symptoms', *British Journal of Educational Psychology*, 48, pp. 159–167.

Laing, R., Phillipson, H. and Lee, A. (1966) *Interpersonal Perception*, London: Tavistock.

Lazarus, R. (1966) *Psychological Stress and the Coping Process*, New York: McGraw-Hill.

Levine, J. and Wang, C. (Eds.) (1983) *Teacher and Student Perceptions: Implications for Learning*, Hillsdale, N.J.: Erlbaum Associates.

Lewin, K. (1947) 'Frontiers in Group Dynamics: Concept, Method and Reality in Social Science; Social Equilibrium and Change', *Human Relations*, 1. No. 1. June, pp. 5–41.

Lewis, J. (1985) 'The Theoretical Underpinnings of School Change Strategies', in Reynolds, D. (Ed.) *Studying School Effectiveness*, Lewes: Falmer.

Lickona, T. (Ed.) (1976) *Moral Development and Behaviour*, New York: Holt, Rinehart and Winston.

Lieberman, A. and Miller, L. (1979) *Staff Development: New Demands, New Realities, New Perspectives*, New York: Teachers College, Columbia University.

Lieberman, M., Yalom, I. and Miles, M. (1973) *Encounter Groups: First Facts*, New York: Basic Books.

Lorac, C. and Weiss, M. (1981) *Communication and Social Skills*, Exeter: Wheaton.

Luce, R. and Raiffa, H. (1957) *Games and Decisions: Introduction and Critical Survey*, New York: Wiley.

Mannheim, K. (1936) *Ideology and Utopia: An Introduction to the Sociology of Knowledge*, Translated by Wirth, L. and Shils, E., New York: Harcourt Brace and Co.

Mannheim, K. (1956) *Essays on the Sociology of Culture*, Edited by Mannheim, E. and Kecskemeti, P., New York: Oxford University Press.

Marland, M. (1974) *Pastoral Care*, London: Heinemann.

Marland, M. (Ed.) (1981) *Information Skills in the Secondary School*, London: Methuen.

Marland, M. (1987) 'Appraisal and Evaluation: Chimera, Fantasy or Practicality?', in Bunnell, S. (Ed.) *Teacher Appraisal in Practice*, London: Heinemann.

Martin, J. (1987) *Cognitive Instructional Counseling*, London, Ontario: Althouse Press.

Matza, D. (1969) *Becoming Deviant*, Englewood Cliffs, N.J.: Prentice Hall.

McCombs, B. (1988) 'Motivational Skills Training: Combining Metacognitive, Cognitive and Affective Learning Strategies', in Weinstein, C., Goetz, E., and Alexander, P. (Eds.) *Learning and Study Strategies*, New York: Academic Press.

McMahon, A., Bolam, R., Abbott, R. and Holly, P. (1984) *Guidelines for Review and Internal Development in Schools*, York: Longman/Schools Council.

Measor, P. and Woods, P. (1984) *Changing Schools*, Milton Keynes: Open University Press.

Melling, A. (1987) Unpublished Dissertation for Certificate of Research Study, Cambridge Institute of Education.

Morgan, A. (1983) 'A Comparative Study of Stress in Remedial and Main Stream Class Teachers', Unpublished M.Ed. Dissertation, Department of Education, University College of Swansea.

Napier, R. and Gershenfeld, M. (1973) *Groups: Theory and Experience*, Boston: Houghton Mifflin.

Nuttall, D. (1981) *School Self-Evaluation*, London: Schools Council.

O'Hara, M. and Jewell, T. (1982) 'Non-Attendance at School: A Behaviourist Approach', in Oldham, *Association of Educational Psychologists Journal*, Vol. 5. No. 8, pp. 28–32.

Oppenheim, A. (1966) *Questionnaire Design and Attitude Measurement*, London: Heinemann.

Osgood, C., Suci, G. and Tannenbaum, P. (1957) *The Measurement of Meaning*, Urbana: University of Illinois Press.

Paisey, A. (1984) *The Effective Teacher*, London: Ward Lock.

Parlett, M. and Hamilton, P. (1972) *Evaluation as Illumination*. Occasional Paper, 9, Edinburgh: Centre for Research in the Educational Sciences.

Parsons, T. and Shils, E. (1951) (Eds.) *Toward a Theory of Action*, Cambridge: Harvard University Press.

Perls, F. (1969) *Gestalt Therapy Verbatim*, New York: Real People Press.

Perls, F., Hefferline, R. and Goodman, P. (1965) *Gestalt Therapy*, New York: Dell.

Phares, E. (1976) *Locus of Control in Personality*, Morriston, N.J.: General Learning Press.

Phillips, B. (1978) *School Stress and Anxiety*, New York: Human Sciences Press.

Piper and Glatter (1977) Cited in Bradley, J., Chesson, R. and Silverleaf, J. (1983) *Inside Staff Development*, Windsor: NFER.

Pruitt, D. (1981) *Negotiation Behaviour*, New York: Academic Press.

Radloff, R. (1968) 'Affiliation and Social Comparison', in Borgatta, E. and Lambert, W. (Eds.) *Handbook of Personality Theory and Research*, Chicago: Rand McNally.

Rapoport, A. and Chammah, A. (1965) *Prisoner's Dilemma: A Study in Conflict and Co-operation*, Ann Arbor: University of Michigan Press.

Read, H. (1958) *Education Through Art*, London: Faber and Faber.

Reddin, W. (1970) *Managerial Effectiveness*, New York: McGraw-Hill.

Reid, K., Hopkins, D. and Holly, P. (1987) *Towards the Effective School*, Oxford: Blackwell.

Reynolds, D. (1987) 'Teacher Appraisal and Development: A Review of the Key Issues' *School Organization* Vol 7, No. 2.

Richardson, E. (1973) *The Teacher, the School and the Task of Management*, London: Heinemann.

Rogers, C. (1959) 'A Theory of Therapy, Personality and Interpersonal Relationships as Developed in the Client-Centered Framework', in Koch, S. (Ed.) *Psychology: A Study of a Science*, Vol. 3. New York: McGraw-Hill.

Rogers, C. (1961) *On Becoming a Person*, Boston: Houghton Mifflin.

Rokeach, M. (1960) *The Open and Closed Mind*, New York: Basic Books.

Rommetweit, R. (1960) *Selectivity, Intuition and Halo Effects in Social Perception*, Oslo: Oslo University Press.

Rose, S. and Edlestone, S. (1987) *Working with Children and Adolescents In Groups*, San Francisco: Jossey-Bass.

Rotter, J., Chance, J. and Phares, E. (1972) *Applications of a Social Learning Theory of Personality*, New York: Holt, Rinehart and Winston.

Rowe, D. (1978) *The Experience of Depression*, Chichester: Wiley.

Rubenowitz, S. (1968) *Emotional Flexibility–Rigidity as a Comprehensive Dimension of Mind*, Stockholm: Almquist and Wiksell.

Rudduck, J. (1980) 'Curriculum change: Management or Meaning?', *School Organization*, Vol. 6, No. 2.

Ruebusch, B. (1966) 'Conceptual Issues, Major Theoretical Approaches, Methodology, Behavioral Correlates of Anxiety', in Stevenson, H. (Ed.) *Sixty second Year Book, National Society for the Study of Education*, Part One, Chicago: Chicago University Press.

Rutter, M., Maugham, B., Mortimore, P. and Ouston, J. (1979) *Fifteen Thousand Hours*, London: Open Books.

Schmuck, R. and Runkel, P. (1985) *The Handbook of Organization Development in Schools*, Palo Alto: Mayfield Publishing.

Sears, D. and Whiting, R. (1973) 'Political Persuasion', in Pool, I. *et al* (Eds.) *Handbook of Communication*, Chicago: Rand McNally.

Smith, R. (1976) *Learning How to Learn in Adult Education*, Department of Secondary and Adult Education, De Kalb: Northern Illinois University.

Somekh, B., Norman, A., Shannon, B. and Abbot, G. (Eds.) (1987) *Action Research in Development*, CARN Bulletin No. 8. Cambridge Institute of Education.

Somerset County Council and Focus in Education (1988) *Let's Get It Right. An Introduction to Teacher Appraisal in Somerset*, Taunton: Somerset County Council.

Spielberger, C. (1966) *Anxiety and Behavior*, New York: Academic Press.

Stanworth, M. (1983) *Gender and Schooling*, London: Hutchinson.

Sumner, R. and Warburton, F. (1972) *Achievement in Secondary School*, Slough: NFER.

Sutcliffe, J. and Whitfield, R. (1979) 'Classroom-Based Teaching Decisions', in Eggleston, J. (Ed.) *Teacher Decision-Making in the Classroom*, London: Routledge and Kegan Paul.

Taylor, M. (1979) 'Teachers' Implicit Personality Systems: An Exploratory Study', in Egglestone, J. (Ed.) (See above).

Thoresen, C. and Mahoney, M. (1974) *Behavioural Self-Control*, New York: Holt, Rinehart and Winston.

Topping, K. (1983) *Educational Systems for Disruptive Adolescents*, London: Croom Helm.

Turner, A. (1987) 'Approach of a School Management Team: A Case Study of a Comprehensive School', *School Organization*, Vol. 7. No. 2.

Tyler, L. (1960) 'Minimum Change Therapy', *Personnel Guidance Journal*, 38, pp. 475–479.

Tyler, L. (1969) *The Work of the Counselor*, New York: Appleton-Century-Crofts.

Wall, W. (1948) *The Adolescent Child*, London: Methuen.

Warwick, D. (1983) *Staff Appraisal*, London: Industrial Society.

Watkins, C. and Wagner, P. (1987) *School Discipline*, Oxford: Blackwell.

Watson, G. and Glaser, E. (1964) *Watson–Glaser Critical Thinking Appraisal Manual*, New York: Harcourt and Brace.

Weinstein, C., Goetz, E. and Alexander, P. (Eds.) (1988) *Learning and Study Strategies*, New York: Academic Press.

Whitehead, N. (1959) *The Aims of Education*, New York: Macmillan.

Wideen, M. and Andrews, I. (1987) *Staff Development for School Improvement*, Lewes: Falmer.

Williams, D. (1981) 'Management of Innovation in Pastoral Care', in Hamblin D. (Ed.) *Problems and Practice of Pastoral Care*, Oxford: Blackwell.

Williams, N. and Williams, S. (1970) *The Moral Development of Children*, London: Macmillan.

Winograd, P. and Hare, V. (1988) 'Reading Comprehension Strategies', in Weinstein, C. *et al*. (See above.)

Woods, P. (Ed.) (1980) *Pupil Strategies*, London: Croom Helm.

Woods, P. (Ed.) (1980) *Teacher Strategies*, London: Croom Helm.

Woods, P. (1985) 'Pupil Strategies', in Bennett, N. and Desforges, C. (Eds.) *Recent Advances in Classroom Research*, Edinburgh: Scottish Academic Press.

Wright, D. (1971) *The Psychology of Moral Behaviour*, Harmondsworth: Penguin.

Index

Subject index

Name index